From Strategy to Revenue

Turning GTM Planning, Sales Execution and Enablement into Measurable Growth

JUAN IGNACIO ELIAS

Published in the United States of America

ISBN 979-8-9932839-1-3 (Paperback)

ISBN 979-8-9932839-2-0 (Hardcover)

ISBN 979-8-9932839-0-6 (eBook)

Cover design by Maria Carolina Elias

Interior design by Juan Ignacio Elias

This book is a work of nonfiction. The information is based on the author's experiences, research, and professional judgment. While every effort has been made to ensure the accuracy of the information contained herein, the book is provided "as is" without warranty of any kind, express or implied. The author shall not be liable for any damages arising from the use of this book. Readers are encouraged to adapt strategies to their own circumstances and consult appropriate professionals where necessary.

Library of Congress Cataloging-in-Publication Data

Elias, Juan Ignacio.

From Strategy to Revenue: Turning GTM Planning, Sales Execution and Enablement into Measurable Growth / Juan Ignacio Elias.

Includes bibliographical references and index.

Library of Congress Control Number: 2025920844

Identifiers: ISBN 979-8-9932839-1-3 (pbk.) | 979-8-9932839-2-0 (hbk.) | 979-8-9932839-0-6 (ebook)

Subjects: LCSH: Sales management. | Marketing Management. | Revenue management. | Industrial management.

First Edition

Printed in the United States of America.

Dedicated to Anabella, Juan Pedro, Francisco and Trinidad, who inspire me on every step I take.

Table of Contents

Foreword

This book is the result of my experience working in commercial functions and consulting for companies across SaaS, technology, and industrial sectors, where I learned firsthand that the real driver of go-to-market (GTM) success is the alignment and coordination of planning, execution, and enablement. Over that time, I've seen repeating patterns; successes that scaled effortlessly, and missteps that quietly eroded performance. What consistently stood out was how quickly growth faltered when these pillars operated in silos, and how dramatically results accelerated when they were connected.

Drawing from over two decades of hands-on leadership, I distill lessons learned from scaling revenue operations and enablement teams globally. With case studies, diagnostic checklists, templates, and practical tools, this book equips you to connect the dots between GTM strategy and execution.

Written for CROs, RevOps leaders, Sales Enablement professionals, and B2B executives, it provides principles, frameworks, and step-by-step playbooks that turn concepts into usable assets. You'll find ready-to-apply models for market segmentation, pipeline management, enablement programs, and GTM scorecards, all designed to help transform GTM execution from a patchwork of initiatives into a coordinated system for growth.

Whether you're building a revenue engine from scratch or modernizing a global organization, you'll find guidance to create the alignment, discipline, and systems your GTM strategy needs to deliver results.

How to Use This Book

You can read this book cover to cover, following the sequence from GTM Planning through Sales Execution to Revenue Enablement, building a complete understanding of how the parts connect. Or you can jump directly to the chapter or section most relevant to your immediate challenge. Each chapter is written to stand alone, but together they form an integrated operating system for GTM excellence.

Introduction: Why GTM Breaks Down

A new fiscal year kicks off. Leadership rolls out the annual sales plan; ambitious targets, new segment focus, a revamped product line. Sales leaders digest the numbers, nod along, and leave the room with marching orders. Meanwhile, Enablement teams scramble to prep content for kickoff, while RevOps works double-time to finalize territories and get quotas loaded into CRM. Everyone is moving fast. Everyone is working hard.

But by Q2, cracks begin to show.

The sales strategy is sound... On paper. The plan defined where to play, but not how to win. Field teams are chasing the right logos with the wrong plays. Reps are struggling to position value, ramp times are dragging, and the pipeline looks wide but shallow. Forecasts start slipping. Everyone feels the pressure.

It's not a talent issue. It's not a tool issue. It's a connectivity issue.

Across B2B organizations, there's a persistent gap between planning, execution, and enablement. These functions should form a continuous loop: strategy shaping actions, execution informing strategy, enablement scaling both. Instead, they operate in silos. Planning is treated as an event, not a system. Execution is reduced to dashboard reviews. Enablement becomes a reactive service desk. The system breaks, quietly but predictably.

This book is about fixing that.

It's about building a modern, integrated GTM operating system that anchors on three essential pillars:

- **GTM Planning:** How to define market opportunity, segment it intelligently, and align resources where they'll yield impact.

- **Sales Execution:** How to drive consistent, high-performance sales behavior through disciplined process and field leadership.

- **Revenue Enablement:** How to scale readiness, skills, and productivity across roles through targeted, embedded enablement.

This book isn't about best practices for a perfect world. It's about what actually works in the messiness of growth.

If you've ever sat in a QBR wondering how your well-designed strategy became unrecognizable in the field, or why reps keep missing the mark despite all the training and tools, you're not alone. You're also not powerless.

Let's connect the dots. Let's rebuild the system. Let's get to work.

Part I: GTM Planning

Chapter 1: Defining the Market You Can Win

"If you don't know exactly where you're aiming, don't be surprised when you miss."

Most GTM failures don't begin in the field, they start in the war room. In countless boardrooms, leadership teams get excited by visions of massive opportunity but gloss over the uncomfortable details: Who will we truly serve? Where will we win first? Which battles are worth fighting now versus later? Without precise targeting, execution becomes a scattershot of campaigns, pitches, and resource allocation that leaves everyone exhausted and revenue goals unmet.

A critical factor often overlooked is that most companies already have a rough sense of where their product or service resonates (e.g., certain industries, problems, or use cases where the fit feels strongest). The challenge isn't guessing where that fit might be; it's quantifying the size of the prize. How large is the true opportunity in those verticals? How much budget is really in play? This is where many organizations stumble, because instinct and anecdotes need to be translated into market sizing. That's what makes moving from vague fit to a disciplined view of your market potential so important.

The discipline of defining your winnable market is not about dampening ambition; it's about channeling it. The goal is to focus your firepower where it creates disproportionate returns, so every sales call, Marketing dollar, and product feature moves you closer to a defensible position in the market.

The Illusion of TAM

Executives love TAM slides. Big numbers look impressive, investors nod, boards get excited. But a $10B TAM means nothing if your product, pricing, and selling motion can only credibly address a fraction of it. That's why it's critical to distinguish between TAM, SAM, and SOM:

- **TAM** (Total Addressable Market) represents the total demand for a product or service if you could capture 100% of the available market. It is a top-down measure of potential, typically expressed in revenue, units, or customers, and serves as the broadest view of opportunity before narrowing to serviceable and obtainable segments.

- **SAM** (Serviceable Available Market) is the portion of the TAM that you can serve with your current products, pricing, and business model.

- **SOM** (Serviceable Obtainable Market) is the subset of the SAM that you can realistically capture given your sales capacity, resources, and competitive dynamics.

Effective planning starts by grounding TAM in reality, translating it into SAM and SOM, and then turning that theoretical spend into an actionable playbook.

In other words:

- **TAM**: Total theoretical market spend in your space

- **SAM**: Subset your current product, pricing, and GTM model can serve

- **SOM**: What your sales team can realistically go after now, given capacity and constraints

Your true growth strategy lives in that last slice (SOM). This is where the magic happens; and it's almost always smaller, more focused, and more profitable than leadership assumes.

From Segmentation to Prioritization

Not all customers are created equal. The best GTM organizations know that the more precisely they define their ideal segments, the more efficient and effective their selling motion becomes.

A robust segmentation model blends:

- **Firmographics**: Industry, size, geography, growth

- **Technographics**: Installed systems, digital maturity

- **Behavioral**: Buying signals, engagement levels

· **Needs-based**: Pain points, regulatory drivers, operational complexity

Then, map these segments against historical performance, win rates, and sales cycle length to prioritize pockets of advantage.

Getting Real About ICP

An Ideal Customer Profile (ICP) is a detailed description of the type of company that is the best fit for your product or service, based on where you have the highest likelihood of winning and creating value. It defines the characteristics of organizations that will benefit most from your offering and deliver the best return on your GTM efforts.

A practical ICP contains:

· Pain/problem statements aligned to your solution

· Clear buying roles and decision paths

· Average deal size and win-rate benchmarks

· Product or integration fit considerations

Your ICP should be a living profile, built from where you've already won and continuously refined.

Example: For a B2B SaaS company offering compliance automation, the ICP might be: "North American financial services firms with 200–2,000 employees, using legacy compliance software, showing signs of scaling compliance teams, with a VP of Compliance as economic buyer and IT Security as technical evaluator, average deal size $75K, historical win rate above 35%, and high integration compatibility with Microsoft 365 and Salesforce."

Buying Personas: Bringing the ICP to Life

While the ICP defines the type of company to target, buying personas drill down into the human decision-makers within those companies. A persona captures role-specific goals, challenges, decision criteria, and preferred engagement styles.

Example Personas for the Compliance Automation ICP:

- **VP of Compliance (Economic Buyer):** Prioritizes risk reduction, efficiency, and audit readiness. Looks for solutions with proven ROI and strong reference customers.

- **IT Security Manager (Technical Evaluator):** Concerned with integration complexity, security certifications, and vendor support responsiveness.

- **Operations Director (Champion):** Focuses on ease of use, automation of manual tasks, and minimal disruption to current workflows.

Defining personas ensures your messaging, content, and sales plays resonate at the individual level, increasing deal velocity and win rates.

Aligning to the Buyer Journey

Your GTM plan must address each of the buyer's core questions, which form the mental checkpoints buyers pass before committing:

- **Why should I care?** Establish relevance and connect to a pressing business problem.

- **Why change now?** Build urgency by highlighting cost of inaction or new opportunities.

- **Why you?** Differentiate through unique value, fit, and trust.

Now, you may have different buyers (personas) who influence the purchasing decision. Each persona you target will answer these questions differently. For the same personas covered in the previous example, this could look like this:

Persona	Why should I care?	Why change now?	Why you?	Why not wait?
VP of Compliance (Economic Buyer)	Risk mitigation, audit readiness	Upcoming regulatory deadline	Proven track record in financial services	Delaying could result in compliance fines
IT Security Manager (Technical Evaluator)	System vulnerabilities, integration gaps	Pending IT upgrade cycle	Certified integrations, robust security	Waiting risks compatibility issues

Persona	Why should I care?	Why change now?	Why you?	Why not wait?
Operations Director (Champion)	Efficiency gains, workload reduction	Staff turnover impacting throughput	User-friendly workflows, quick onboarding	Delay prolongs inefficiencies

Map messaging, plays, and engagement to **Awareness**, **Evaluation**, and **Decision** phases, tailoring content and approach to each persona's lens on these core questions.

Organizational Implications

Clear segments and ICPs should directly shape the design and execution of your commercial model. When you know precisely who you're targeting and why, you can allocate resources in a way that maximizes impact and minimizes waste. This is where strategic intent turns into practical, day-to-day decisions:

- **Territory design:** Assign coverage based on market potential, segment concentration, and buying patterns rather than arbitrary geographies or legacy assignments.

- **Quota allocation:** Tie quotas to real opportunity within each segment or territory, balancing stretch with achievability to sustain motivation and avoid sandbagging.

- **Campaign strategy:** Focus Marketing and sales plays where the ICP fit is strongest, customizing content, channels, and offers for each segment.

- **Partner strategy:** Select and enable partners whose reach, expertise, and relationships map directly to your highest-priority segments.

In practice, this might mean shifting headcount toward emerging high-fit segments, reconfiguring account assignments to concentrate expertise, or creating specialized campaigns for verticals where your win rates and expansion potential are highest. The tighter the link between segmentation/ICP insights and operational levers, the more consistently you'll outperform competitors who spread themselves too thin.

Wrap-Up: Planning for Precision

Defining the market you can win isn't a once-a-year deck. It's an ongoing process of refinement. It means rejecting one-size-fits-all models in favor of precision. It requires Finance, RevOps, Marketing, Product, and Sales to work together; not in parallel, but in lockstep.

In the next chapter, we'll go deeper into buyer journey mapping, because knowing *who* to target is just the start. You also need to know *how* they buy and what moves them to act.

Chapter 2: Crafting a Buyer-Centric Value Proposition

"The value of an idea lies in the using of it." Thomas Edison

Why Value Proposition Matters

Defining the market you can win is the first crucial step in GTM planning. It provides the guardrails: the boundaries of opportunity, the size of the prize, and the profile of the customers worth pursuing. But identifying the right market is not enough. The next step is to answer the essential question: **Why should those customers choose you over the alternatives?**

That is where your value proposition comes in. A compelling value proposition translates your strategy into a clear, buyer-centric promise of outcomes. It is the bridge between defining a market and mapping the buyer journey. Without it, segmentation and ICP exercises remain theoretical, disconnected from the realities of customer choice. With it, every function -from Sales to Marketing to Customer Success- can align around a shared narrative of value.

What a Value Proposition Is (and Isn't)

A value proposition is not a tagline, slogan, or product pitch. It is the articulation of the unique, defensible, and customer-relevant benefits you deliver. More importantly, it is the narrative glue that connects your strategy to the customer's reality. When crafted well, it becomes a north star that guides every sales conversation, marketing campaign, and customer success interaction. It should:

· Speak directly to the **problems and priorities of your ICP**, showing that you understand their world and the pressures they face.

· Translate features into **measurable business outcomes**, such as revenue growth, cost savings, or risk reduction.

- **Differentiate your offering from your competitors'** in a way that is sustainable and credible, highlighting strengths that matter most to buyers.

- **Be simple enough for every seller to repeat in the field**, and strong enough for every buyer to believe and champion internally.

Weak value propositions sound like generic claims that could apply to anyone, anywhere (e.g., "We help companies grow faster"). They fail because they are too broad and lack proof.

Strong ones, by contrast, are specific, differentiated, and provable. For example: "We help mid-market manufacturers reduce unplanned downtime by 25% through predictive maintenance analytics, improving EBITDA by an average of $5M annually." These statements resonate because they tie the solution directly to measurable impact and give the customer confidence in your ability to deliver.

Defining Value and Tying It to Messaging

Before diving into frameworks, it is important to pause and define what "value" means in the context of GTM. Value is the intersection between customer pain points, the outcomes they seek, and the differentiated capabilities your solution delivers. Defining value is not just about the product; it is about the impact on the customer's business and the story you consistently tell in the market. It should connect to the challenges executives care about (i.e, growth, profitability, risk) and make the link between your offering and those business imperatives explicit.

When articulated effectively, defined value becomes the foundation for messaging. It ensures that your campaigns, sales conversations, and customer success narratives all reinforce the same story. Strong messaging ties features to outcomes, highlights differentiation, and speaks the customer's language rather than internal jargon. It also creates coherence across functions: Marketing introduces the narrative, sales validates it in conversation, and customer success proves it through delivery. For example:

- **Weak messaging**: "Our platform automates workflows with cutting-edge AI." This is company-centric, technology-first, and disconnected from impact.

· **Strong messaging**: "We help HR leaders cut onboarding time in half by automating manual processes, freeing up managers to focus on retention and culture." This is buyer-centric, outcome-oriented, and grounded in measurable results.

Organizations that excel at this translation from value definition to messaging often build internal playbooks with messaging pillars, customer proof points, and objection-handling guides, ensuring that every touchpoint reinforces the same value story.

Frameworks to Define Value

There are multiple frameworks leaders can use to ensure their value proposition is grounded in the buyer's perspective. Each provides a different lens through which to analyze how value is created and communicated. Here are some examples:

· **Jobs-to-Be-Done (JTBD):** Focus on the progress your customers are trying to make, not just the product they buy. What "job" are they hiring your solution to do? This framework pushes teams to think beyond features and into outcomes customers care about, such as saving time, reducing complexity, or unlocking new growth.

· **Value Pyramid (Bain & Co.):** Identify the level of value your solution delivers -functional (cost, time savings), emotional (reduced risk, confidence), or strategic (growth, innovation, market leadership)-. Many offerings begin at the functional level, but sustainable differentiation usually requires moving higher up the pyramid into emotional and strategic impact.

· **Outcome-Based Messaging:** Anchor your value to quantifiable results (i.e., ROI, revenue impact, cost reduction, compliance, or risk mitigation). Translate product attributes into buyer outcomes and quantify them whenever possible. For instance, instead of saying a platform "improves collaboration," demonstrate how it shortens project timelines by 30% and reduces rework costs by $2M annually.

These frameworks are not mutually exclusive. High-performing GTM organizations often combine these approaches: using JTBD to clarify the customer's underlying goals, the Value Pyramid to elevate the conversation, and outcome-based messaging to provide the proof points that make the story credible.

Testing and Validating Your Value Proposition

A value proposition is only as strong as its proof. Without validation, even the most well-crafted narrative risks being dismissed as Marketing spin. Buyers are skeptical by default; they expect evidence, outcomes, and real-world results to back up bold claims. Validation is how you demonstrate credibility, build trust, and ensure that your value story resonates not just in theory but in practice.

Validation requires:

- **Voice of Customer:** Interviews, win/loss analysis, and customer success stories. Go beyond anecdotes to capture themes across multiple accounts, ensuring the voice of the customer is systematically integrated into product and GTM decisions.

- **Quantification:** ROI calculators, case studies, and benchmarks. Hard numbers resonate with executives; when you can say, "On average, our solution pays for itself in six months," the value prop becomes tangible and credible.

- **Competitive Differentiation:** Understanding where you truly win and where you must catch up. This requires continuous intelligence on competitor strengths and weaknesses, so your teams know exactly how to position and defend your edge.

Validation should be iterative, not a one-time event. Organizations that continually test and refine their value proposition -through pilots, customer councils, and data-driven insights- ensure it remains relevant as markets evolve. This process transforms your value proposition from an internal hypothesis into a tested customer truth, one that is proven in the field and reinforced by evidence.

Translating Value into GTM Execution

Once defined, your value proposition becomes the foundation for execution. It is not a static statement tucked into a strategy deck; it should be a living, breathing part of your GTM system's daily operations. The power of a well-crafted value prop is that it becomes a through-line, ensuring that every function reinforces the same promise of value to the customer.

- **Sales Process:** Every stage of discovery, qualification, and proposal should tie back to customer outcomes. Discovery questions should probe for impact areas linked to your value prop, and proposals should explicitly show how your solution delivers those outcomes.

- **Enablement:** Reps must be trained to sell value, not features, anchoring conversations on buyer priorities. This includes role plays, objection handling tied to your differentiation, and reinforcement through manager coaching.

- **Marketing Alignment:** Campaigns, content, and messaging must consistently reinforce the value proposition. Strong alignment ensures that what a prospect reads in a whitepaper matches what they hear from a rep and what they later experience in onboarding.

- **Customer Success:** Post-sale, your team must ensure that promised value is delivered, reinforced, and expanded. Success plans should map explicitly to the outcomes promised in the value proposition, creating a closed loop from pitch to proof.

When these functions are aligned around the same value promise, execution becomes more consistent, trust with customers is strengthened, and expansion opportunities naturally emerge.

Making It Measurable

A value proposition is dynamic. It must evolve with customer needs, competitive landscapes, and proof points. Treating it as a static statement risks irrelevance; what resonates with buyers today may not tomorrow. That is why measurement and feedback are critical: they allow you to test whether your value story is still compelling and adjust accordingly.

To ensure it remains relevant, tie it to measurable outcomes such as:

- **Win rate within ICP segments:** Rising or falling win rates are often the most direct signal of whether your value resonates in the market.

· **Sales cycle length compared to competitors:** A stronger, clearer value proposition tends to shorten cycles by accelerating customer conviction.

· **Retention and expansion rates tied to value realization**: If customers renew and grow, it is proof that your promise translates into actual impact.

· **Customer satisfaction (NPS, CSAT) connected to outcomes delivered**: High scores that reference business results are strong validation of your value story.

Feedback loops from these metrics should feed back into GTM planning, ensuring your value proposition is continuously refined. Leading organizations even formalize this by conducting quarterly value reviews, where product, Marketing, Sales, and Customer Success teams examine evidence and update messaging or proof points. This discipline turns measurement into a competitive advantage, making your value proposition both credible and adaptable.

Wrap Up

Defining your addressable market tells you *where to play*. Your value proposition tells you *why you can win*. Together, they form the foundation for mapping the buyer journey and building execution discipline. They also create the context for every decision that follows in GTM: how you invest in channels, what plays you prioritize, and how you enable your teams. A buyer-centric value proposition ensures that every message, motion, and metric in your GTM system is oriented toward the same outcome: delivering differentiated value that customers believe in and are willing to pay for. Ultimately, this is what transforms a strategy on paper into traction in the market and revenue growth that sustains over time.

Chapter 3: Mapping the Buyer Journey

"You don't sell when you're ready. You sell when they are."

Understanding the buyer journey isn't just a Marketing exercise. It's foundational to GTM success. Too often, companies design plans around **what** they want to sell and **when** they want to push it. That perspective is inside-out. The best GTM leaders flip the lens to outside-in: they begin by studying how buyers actually make decisions, what questions they ask, and what frictions slow them down. Then they align everything - messaging, plays, process, enablement, even compensation levers- to that journey.

The difference is dramatic. When you sell on your own schedule, you risk missing the real moments of influence. When you sell on the buyer's schedule, you create relevance, trust, and velocity. This chapter is about closing that gap, bridging how companies want to sell with how customers truly buy, and making sure every interaction meets the buyer where they are, not where you wish they were.

The Myth of the Linear Journey

Traditional funnel diagrams paint a neat, linear picture:

Awareness → Consideration → Decision → Purchase

But modern B2B buying isn't that clean. Multiple stakeholders, shifting internal priorities, budget cycles, risk aversion, and competitive noise all make the real journey messy and non-linear. Deals often feel more like navigating a maze than moving down a funnel.

Buyers today:

· **Loop between stages multiple times** as priorities change or new objections arise.

· **Frequently pause** or restart their evaluation when budgets shift or leadership turns over.

- **Bring in new stakeholders mid-cycle**, altering requirements and consensus dynamics.

- **Compare multiple solutions in parallel**, weighing trade-offs across vendors.

- **Seek validation** through peer reviews, analysts, and informal networks before committing.

For sellers, this means that influence must be earned at every turn, not just at the "decision" stage. Content, plays, and conversations need to anticipate backtracking, stalls, and sudden expansions of the buying group. If your GTM strategy assumes a straight line from "lead" to "close," you're already misaligned and at risk of losing deals to more adaptive competitors.

Identifying Buying Jobs, Not Just Stages

Reframing the buyer journey around **buyer jobs** -the tasks they need to complete to move forward- is more actionable than static funnel stages. By thinking in terms of jobs-to-be-done, you shift from managing pipeline milestones to solving real progress blockers buyers face.

Typical buying jobs include:

- **Diagnosing a pain** or opportunity, often led by operators or functional managers who feel the problem day-to-day.

- **Building internal alignment** and urgency, typically championed by a business sponsor who must rally consensus across skeptical peers.

- **Exploring solution categories**, where technical evaluators and analysts benchmark options and frame requirements.

- **Gaining confidence in specific vendors**, as economic buyers and influencers compare credibility, references, and fit.

- **Quantifying ROI** and building the business case, often owned by Finance leaders and executive sponsors who need hard numbers.

- **Navigating procurement or legal processes**, led by procurement teams who balance risk, compliance, and cost.

Different stakeholders own different jobs, and each job carries distinct risks if left unresolved. For example, if internal alignment isn't achieved, even the best product fit will stall. If procurement hurdles aren't anticipated, deals will drag late in the cycle. Your GTM must address each job: **who does it, what's at stake, what obstacles are common, and how you help overcome them**. By mapping jobs in this way, you empower reps to act as guides, removing friction and accelerating buyer progress.

Buyer Roles & Influence Maps

Enterprise deals rarely involve a single decision-maker. A successful GTM plan must consider the **full cast of characters**, each of whom views risk and value through a different lens:

- **Economic buyers:** Care about ROI, risk, and strategic alignment. They want proof that the investment moves the business forward and that the vendor will be around to support long-term goals.

- **Technical evaluators:** Focus on integrations, security, and scalability. They are the gatekeepers of feasibility and often hold veto power if requirements aren't met.

- **Champions:** Advocate internally but need credibility and clarity from you to convince others. They are the bridge between your solution and the internal buying committee.

- **End users:** Care about ease of use and daily workflows. If they see your product as cumbersome, adoption and expansion will stall, even if leadership approves.

- **Procurement/legal:** Gatekeepers on process, risk, and price. Their role is to protect the company, which means you must anticipate their objections and build in time for negotiation.

Map their roles, pain points, and decision influence. Then align your messaging, plays, and rep engagement strategy accordingly. The most effective GTM leaders go further, building influence maps that show who trusts whom, where alliances or friction exist, and how information flows within the account. This level of visibility turns a deal from guesswork into a coordinated strategy.

Triggers and Inflection Points

Understand **what causes a buyer to enter or re-enter the journey**. These triggers are gold for targeting and campaign design. They represent moments of vulnerability or urgency when the status quo is being questioned and buyers are most open to new perspectives. Effective GTM teams study these signals obsessively, building plays, content, and outreach sequences that land exactly when buyers are seeking answers.

Examples:

· **New executive hired**: often brings fresh priorities and openness to change.

· **Regulatory change**: creates urgency to comply, with risk of fines or penalties.

· **Budget cycle resets**: windows when funding can be unlocked if the business case is timely.

· **Failed initiative**: buyers are looking for alternatives, credibility matters.

· **Customer complaint or churn event**: heightens the need to fix gaps before damage spreads.

· **Product launch or market shift**: sparks competitive pressure or opens new opportunities.

Design GTM motions around these trigger events. Your ability to show up with relevance at the right moment is what creates velocity. Great GTM teams don't just react to triggers... They anticipate them by monitoring intent data, industry news, customer signals, and executive moves, then orchestrating outreach so that when the moment arrives, they are the first and most credible voice at the table.

Content and Plays Aligned to the Journey

For each buyer job or stage, define not only the mechanics of content but also the psychology of progression. Think about what is happening in the buyer's world at that point, and how you can reduce risk or friction for them.

· **Key questions they're asking:** What uncertainties or doubts dominate their thinking right now?

· **What they need to believe to move forward**: The mental shift required to take the next step.

· **The role sales needs to play:** Are you a challenger, a coach, a consultant, or a problem-solver?

· **The assets and plays needed to support it**: Tools, proof points, or stories that provide confidence.

Example:

Buyer Job	Sales Role	Assets/Plays	Narrative to Emphasize
Build urgency	Challenger	Industry trends deck, impact calculator	"The cost of doing nothing is higher than change."
Evaluate options	Trusted advisor	Competitive battlecards, product demo	"Here's how we stack up, and why that matters."
Gain internal alignment	Coach	Executive one-pager, quantified value story	"This is the story you can take to your CFO."
Navigate procurement	Partner	ROI models, case studies, contract playbook	"We've done this before, here's how to de-risk it."

This alignment is what turns content into conversion, not just more PDFs in a library. When content is mapped to buyer jobs with clarity of role, belief, and narrative, every asset becomes a lever to move deals forward with intention.

Implications for GTM Execution

Buyer journey mapping isn't just a planning tool. It's the connective tissue between strategy and day-to-day execution. Done well, it ensures that every GTM function is oriented around how buyers actually move, not how internal teams wish they would. It drives alignment, reduces wasted effort, and creates a consistent customer experience.

· **Sales process design:** Stages should mirror buying behavior, not internal steps. This keeps forecasting grounded in reality and avoids premature stage progression.

· **Sales training:** Equip reps to diagnose where buyers are and guide them forward. Role plays, call coaching, and deal reviews should all reference buyer jobs, not just pipeline stages.

· **Marketing strategy:** Match campaign content to buyer jobs and triggers. This ensures demand generation feels timely and relevant, increasing conversion rates.

· **Sales tech stack:** Align CRM, engagement tools, and analytics to buyer signals so that frontline teams get alerts and insights tied to real buyer activity, not vanity metrics.

When buyer journey mapping informs execution, you move from selling at buyers to **selling with them**; a shift that builds trust, accelerates deals, and strengthens long-term relationships.

Example: A SaaS Buyer Journey in Practice

Stage	Key Activities	Expected Outcomes	Roles Involved
Awareness	Prospect reads industry report, attends webinar, sees peer review	Recognition of problem, interest sparked	Marketing, SDR
Problem Diagnosis	Operations team documents inefficiencies, highlights rising costs	Agreement on urgency and scope of issue	Operations Director, Finance, Champion
Solution Exploration	Shortlist vendors, request demos, engage with SEs	Identification of potential vendors and solution categories	IT Security, Procurement, AE, SE
Business Case	Build ROI model, compare cost of status quo vs. change, gather references	Consensus forms, sponsor builds internal business case	VP of Compliance, Finance, Champion, AE
Evaluation & Alignment	Executive briefings, proof-of-concept, internal presentations	Stakeholder alignment, executive sponsorship secured	Economic Buyer, Champion, Technical Evaluators
Decision & Procurement	Negotiations on terms, legal review, risk assessment	Contract signed, deployment planning initiated	Procurement, Legal, AE, SE, Executive Sponsor
Implementation & Value	Onboarding, user training, adoption metrics tracked	Solution goes live, first outcomes delivered	CSM, AM, End Users, Champion

This end-to-end view shows how different personas step in at different moments, what they need to accomplish, and how sellers can help reduce friction at each stage. It connects abstract journey mapping to the lived reality of advancing deals.

Wrap-Up: Sell How They Buy

Mapping the buyer journey forces discipline. It requires you to think from the outside in, resisting the temptation to force buyers into your internal process. When mapped carefully, it provides a common language for sales, Marketing, and Product teams to coordinate around real buyer behavior. Done well, it aligns every part of GTM, from messaging and plays to territory strategy, campaign design, and forecast stages.

Just as importantly, it **should directly shape your internal sales process**: pipeline stages, exit criteria, and forecasting checkpoints must mirror the buyer's progression, not arbitrary internal milestones. You stop guessing where the deal is, because you can tie activity to buyer progress with confidence. It also gives leaders clearer visibility to coach, intervene, and reallocate resources at the right time.

In the next chapter, we'll shift to **Routes-to-Market** and how to determine the right mix of direct, indirect, and digital paths to drive coverage without creating complexity or cost drag.

Chapter 4: Building Your Route-to-Market Strategy

"How you sell should be as strategic as what you sell."

Your Route-to-Market (RTM) is the circulatory system of your commercial engine. It determines how efficiently opportunity flows from market potential into booked revenue. It's the blueprint for connecting your offering with the right customers, in the right way, at the right cost. Many companies over-engineer their product but underthink their path to the customer. They default to what they've always done -field sales, channel partners, inside reps- without assessing whether that path aligns with their buyer's preferences, their market's complexity, or their own cost structure. As a result, they either overpay for revenue or leave markets underserved. Get it wrong, and even the best products stall in the pipeline. Get it right, and you create operating leverage that compounds over time.

The RTM Equation

There's no single "right" route. The right mix depends on four major factors:

- **Coverage needs**: Which markets, how many accounts, and which geographies require attention.

- **Cost-to-serve constraints**: The economics of ACV, margins, and channel costs.

- **Buyer expectations**: How your customers prefer to research, evaluate, and purchase.

- **Sales motion complexity**: Whether the motion is touchless, transactional, or highly consultative.

Ultimately, you are balancing three dimensions:

- **Reach**: Can you effectively cover the right accounts and segments?

- **Fit**: Does your model align with how the buyer wants to engage?

· **Yield**: Is it cost-effective given expected ACV, margins, and sales cycle length?

No route is inherently "better" than another. A field-heavy enterprise motion can be a goldmine for complex, high-ACV deals, and a disaster for low-margin transactional sales. The art is in matching the channel mix to your market context, buyer behavior, and growth priorities.

For example, if buyers expect digital self-serve but you deploy a field-heavy model, you inflate cost-to-serve and frustrate prospects. Conversely, trying to win $500K enterprise deals with a pure PLG motion risks credibility and support gaps.

The most successful companies treat RTM design as a living portfolio: continuously tested, benchmarked, and refined against market signals, win rates, and margin outcomes. Done this way, the route is not only efficient but resilient as buyer expectations, product strategy, and competitive dynamics evolve.

Options and When to Use Them

Before choosing or refining your RTM, it's useful to compare the main options side by side. Each route has clear strengths, risks, and strategic considerations. The table below summarizes when to use each approach and what to watch for:

Route	Use When...	Watchouts	Strategic Considerations
Field Sales	High ACV, complex, relationship-heavy	High cost-to-serve	Best for strategic accounts where executive access and customization are critical
Inside Sales	Mid ACV, repeatable, regional coverage	Requires tight Marketing alignment	Works well for scalable outreach, provided pipeline is well-qualified
Digital / PLG	Low ACV, high velocity, self-service	Needs strong product instrumentation	Ideal for SaaS or transactional models where speed and ease drive adoption
Channel	Fragmented markets, new geos	Conflict risk, low pipeline visibility	Extends reach efficiently, but success hinges on governance and partner enablement
Alliances	Ecosystem co-selling, complex solutions	Long ramp time, heavy enablement required	Amplifies credibility and reach when paired with established platforms or vendors

The trick isn't picking one, it's picking the **right mix**, then aligning resourcing, incentives, and motion around it. The most effective GTM leaders constantly test this mix, doubling down on what delivers margin and growth while pruning routes that dilute focus.

Avoiding Channel Conflict

Channel conflict is a silent killer of trust and momentum. Multi-channel models break down when the rules of engagement are unclear or when sellers feel like they're fighting each other instead of the competition. What starts as a coverage strategy quickly devolves into finger-pointing, stalled deals, and lost trust from both customers and partners.

Common mistakes:

- **Overlapping territories** between direct teams and partners, leading to double-coverage and confusion.

- **Lack of deal registration** or partner protection, leaving resellers exposed and hesitant to invest.

- **Compensation plans** that create internal competition, rewarding channel conflict instead of collaboration.

To avoid this:

- Define **channel governance**: clearly document who owns which accounts, by segment, territory, or product line

- Ensure **incentive alignment**: design comp neutrality or tiered incentives that make collaboration a win-win

- Build **clear escalation paths**: give reps clarity on when to pull in a partner, when to lead solo, and how disputes are resolved

- Provide **visibility and attribution**: make sure CRM and pipeline reporting give all parties transparency into who is influencing deals

The moment two reps from different motions compete for the same deal without clarity, you introduce politics where there should be pipeline. Customers sense misalignment instantly, and trust erodes quickly. Conversely, when governance and incentives are clear, alignment creates confidence and velocity, turning partners into amplifiers rather than competitors

Vertical and Geo Considerations

Not all markets behave the same. Highly regulated industries often demand a high-touch, relationship-led approach where credibility, compliance expertise, and long-term trust are essential. Emerging geographies may require local language support, on-the-ground partnerships, regulatory navigation, and even different pricing or packaging models to reflect local purchasing power. Mature markets, on the other hand, may value efficiency, digital-first engagement, and sophisticated procurement processes.

This means GTM leaders must avoid the temptation to simply "copy-paste" their home market model. What works in North America may not work in LATAM or APAC. Instead, build segment-first, not legacy-first. Study the regulatory environment, competitive dynamics, and cultural nuances of each market before finalizing your route.

Each RTM decision should flow from segment needs and execution economics, not internal politics or legacy models. The more you adapt coverage, resourcing, and messaging to market realities, the higher the odds of profitable, sustainable growth.

Partner Strategy: Accelerator or Trap

Partners can be your growth accelerators... Or your biggest distraction. A strong partner strategy can rapidly expand reach and reduce CAC (Customer Acquisition Cost). But too many companies launch a channel without doing the hard work of definition and enablement first.

Common gaps include:

- **No clear partner profiles** or tiering to distinguish strategic from opportunistic players.

- **Undefined co-selling motions**, leaving reps unsure of how to collaborate.

- **Weak or absent onboarding and certification**, resulting in unprepared partners.

- **Lack of shared pipeline visibility or attribution**, creating mistrust and finger-pointing.

To succeed, treat partners as an extension of your salesforce, not an afterthought:

- **Define partner profiles and tiers:** Know which partners bring reach, expertise, or credibility, and prioritize accordingly.

- **Structure co-selling motions:** Establish joint objectives, rules of engagement, and shared accountability.

- **Invest in enablement:** Provide onboarding, certification, and ongoing training to build partner confidence.

- **Ensure visibility:** Share pipeline, track attribution, and align on metrics that make performance transparent.

Remember: partners don't "just sell it." They need motivation, support, and inspection, just like your own reps. The most effective partner ecosystems are cultivated deliberately, with governance, incentives, and consistent engagement that make selling together easier than selling alone.

Example - RTM in Action

A mid-market SaaS firm serving financial services firms segmented its motion like this:

Segment	Sales Motion
$100K+ ACV, strategic account:	**Enterprise field sales**
$25K–100K ACV, regional firm	**Inside sales + virtual SEs**
<$25K ACV	**Digital-led motion**, self-service trials + inbound SDR
Expansion into LATAM	**Channel partners** with territory exclusivity and local enablement

The result? 30% YoY growth with improved margin. Not because they sold harder, but because they routed smarter.

Wrap-Up: Design to Win, Not Just to Cover

RTM is not about coverage for its own sake. It's about aligning sales cost, buyer preference, and resource efficiency to unlock profitable growth. A strong RTM design flexes with opportunity, scales as your business evolves, and avoids the traps of over-investing in the wrong channels or underserving priority segments. The best leaders treat RTM as a competitive weapon; one that is continuously monitored, tested, and recalibrated against market signals, win rates, and margin performance.

If your current model doesn't flex to opportunity or scale with your business, it's time to rearchitect. The organizations that outperform are those that treat RTM not as a static choice but as a living system; regularly assessed, optimized, and evolved as buyer expectations and competitive dynamics shift.

Next up: **Territory and Resource Allocation**, because once you've chosen your route, the real test is execution. Success depends on ensuring the right people are focused on the right accounts, with the capacity and incentives to maximize impact. This is where strategic design becomes operational reality.

Chapter 5: Territory & Resource Planning

"Your revenue engine is only as strong as how you allocate its horsepower."

Treat territory and capacity planning as a disciplined, forward-looking design exercise rather than a reactive quarterly scramble. This is the point where your GTM vision collides with operational reality, where you decide who will pursue which opportunities, with what intensity, and at what cost.

The best GTM organizations treat territory and resource planning as a **strategic design decision**, not a quarterly fire drill. They use data, not legacy. And they revisit the model as the market evolves, not just when someone quits.

Four Levers of GTM Resource Design

You have four main design levers when planning rep coverage:

· **Territory** (accounts/regions): define them with precision, balancing potential with manageability

· **Capacity** (accounts a rep can work): right-size workloads to ensure quality engagement

· **Quota** (target tied to potential): match ambition to opportunity to drive focus without burnout

· **Role Mix** (SDR/AE/AM/SE, overlays): configure teams for the specific demands of your motion

Each of these should tie directly back to your market segmentation and RTM strategy, not just geography or legacy assignments.

Territory Design Models

There's no one-size-fits-all approach to territory carving. The right model depends on your GTM motion and customer base.

Common approaches may include:

Model	Best For	Challenges
Geographic	Localized markets	Uneven TAM/deal flow
Named Account	Strategic/ABM	Research-heavy, slower ramp
Industry/Vertical	Regulated/specialized	Requires deep domain expertise
Hybrid	Mid-market/regional enterprise	Complexity/overlap

The best designs use account potential, rep productivity, whitespace analysis, and coverage gaps as primary inputs, not historical comfort zones.

Capacity Planning: Coverage vs. Cost

Not every segment deserves the same level of human touch. To avoid over- or under-resourcing, model:

- **Rep capacity:** How many accounts can a rep realistically cover per week/month?

- **Activity targets:** Based on sales cycle and deal size, what level of activity yields success?

- **Service levels:** Define what kind of touch each tier gets (e.g., field, inside, digital, or partner)

Example:

Segment	Coverage Model
Top-tier strategic accounts	1:1 field coverage
Mid-market	Named rep with quarterly touchpoints
SMB/long-tail	SDR-managed or self-service

This lets you scale without burning out reps or overspending to chase marginal deals. More importantly, it allows you to match the **cost of coverage** with the **value of opportunity**. Enterprise accounts justify deep, bespoke engagement because each deal can be transformative. Mid-market accounts require balance: structured but lighter touches to sustain momentum. SMB or long-tail segments benefit from automation, pooled resources, and digital-first engagement, ensuring you don't apply enterprise-level expense to small-ticket revenue.

Think of capacity planning as dynamic resource allocation rather than static territory design. As markets shift, customer expectations change, and digital tools evolve, you must recalibrate coverage models. Some companies even embed **trigger points**. For example, if deal size in SMB rises by 20% for three quarters, coverage moves from self-service to SDR support. In this way, coverage models become living systems that flex with reality instead of rigid rules carved once a year.

Quota Allocation: Match Risk to Reality

Quota setting is often where strategic rigor gives way to wishful thinking. To set fair and achievable targets, leaders must blend analytical discipline with field-level reality. Quotas should not simply be numbers that close a spreadsheet gap, but commitments that balance opportunity, risk, and motivation.

· Use **bottom-up modeling** (capacity × conversion × ACV) to ground targets in real selling capacity.

· Layer with **top-down expectations** (growth targets by segment) so that quotas align with the company's strategic trajectory.

· Adjust for **ramp time, tenure, and market changes**, recognizing that a new rep in a new territory cannot deliver the same output as a tenured rep in a mature market.

· Validate against **historical attainment** and pipeline data to avoid unrealistic jumps that set reps up for failure.

Quota should reflect territory potential. When done well, quotas create a sense of fairness, stretch without breaking, and provide a motivational compass for both reps and leadership.

They also become a diagnostic tool: consistent misses signal flawed assumptions, while consistent over-attainment may suggest under-assignment of opportunity. In both cases, quota management becomes a feedback loop to improve GTM design.

Role Specialization for Scale

As you scale, complexity increases. That's where role specialization becomes critical. Generalist, full-cycle reps may work in early stages, but at scale they slow you down and dilute focus. Specialization drives both efficiency and depth of expertise.

- **SDRs** for prospecting and lead qualification, ensuring a steady and qualified pipeline.

- **AEs** for new business acquisition, focused solely on advancing and closing opportunities.

- **AMs or CSMs** for expansion and retention, safeguarding the base while driving net revenue retention.

- **Solutions Engineers** or **overlay specialists** for technical depth, ensuring buyers see how the product solves complex, domain-specific challenges.

Clear ownership across the funnel prevents bottlenecks and burnout. Don't make AEs chase renewals, build their own pipeline, and run complex demos. That's not "full-cycle", that's inefficiency disguised as heroism.

Think of specialization not just as role design, but as an operating philosophy. By matching responsibilities to strengths, you create a system where each player knows their lane, executes with excellence, and hands off cleanly. The result is higher velocity, better customer experience, and an organization built for sustained scale.

Redesign Triggers and Cadence

Don't wait for attrition or reorgs to rethink coverage. Re-evaluate when:

- New segments or products launch: coverage must flex with fresh opportunity pools.

· You shift up/down market: enterprise vs. SMB motions demand very different models.

· Performance is uneven across territories: some consistently over-achieve while others struggle, signaling misaligned design.

· You see consistent under/over-capacity signals: either reps are drowning in accounts or under-utilized.

· Major market forces or competitive moves change the landscape: new entrants, regulatory shifts, or disruptive technologies can instantly alter coverage economics.

Annual planning is a minimum. High-growth orgs reassess every 6 months, and some even build quarterly reviews into their operating rhythm. The goal isn't constant churn, but maintaining a living model that evolves with reality instead of waiting until pain points force a disruptive reorg.

Wrap-Up: Design for Growth, Not Politics

Territory and resource planning is where GTM strategy collides with execution. It determines how opportunity is distributed, how capacity is balanced, and how fair performance expectations are set. Missteps here create wasted effort, uneven attainment, and rep frustration. But when done right, coverage is equitable, quotas are credible, and execution starts with clarity and confidence.

The next chapter dives into **Sales Compensation Design**, the lever that translates this design into daily behavior. Incentives, more than any slide deck, shape how the field shows up and where they put their energy.

Chapter 6: Sales Compensation Design

"Show me the comp plan, and I'll show you the strategy."

The transition from coverage and quota design into compensation is intentional. Once you've defined **who** owns which accounts, **how much** capacity they can handle, and **what** their quota should be, the natural next step is deciding **how they get paid**. Compensation is the mechanism that turns all those design choices into frontline behavior.

Compensation is one of the most powerful levers to align rep behavior with company priorities. It deserves its own chapter because it's more than math. It's management philosophy made tangible. A poorly designed plan creates misalignment, sandbagging, and churn. A great plan creates clarity, focus, and momentum.

Core Principles

Before designing or refining a sales compensation plan, it's helpful to anchor on a few guiding principles. These principles act as guardrails to ensure the plan doesn't just work on paper but drives the right behaviors in practice.

- **Align to strategy:** Reward the outcomes that matter most (e.g., expansion, multi-year contracts, new logos). Don't just pay for volume, design incentives that steer reps toward the business's growth priorities.

- **Balance risk and reward:** Mix base and variable pay to drive performance without destabilizing rep earnings. The right risk profile motivates without pushing reps into short-term thinking or excessive stress.

- **Keep it simple:** Reps should be able to calculate commissions themselves. Complexity erodes trust; clarity builds confidence and urgency.

- **Ensure fairness:** Account for territory potential and quota realism. A plan that ignores structural differences between territories quickly becomes a source of attrition and resentment.

- **Evolve annually:** As your GTM shifts, your comp model must too. Just as products, markets, and motions change, so must incentives. What drives the right behavior this year may be misaligned the next. Treat comp as a living mechanism that grows with the business.

Common Structures

Before selecting a specific compensation structure, it's important to understand the common models available and the trade-offs each carries. These structures provide the foundation for how earnings are distributed and how risk and reward are shared between the company and the salesforce.

- **Straight commission**: Simple, but risky for rep retention. It drives pure performance but can create instability and turnover.

- **Base + variable**: Most common, balances stability with motivation. Reps have predictable income with upside tied to results.

- **Tiered accelerators**: Higher payout % as reps surpass quota. This design rewards over-performance and creates momentum near and beyond 100% attainment.

- **Draws and guarantees**: Helpful during ramp periods. They give new hires or new market entrants time to build pipeline without financial stress.

- **SPIFFs and bonuses**: Short-term levers for product launches or behavior shifts. When used sparingly, they provide sharp focus on priorities without distorting the long-term plan.

Role-Specific Design

Different roles influence different parts of the revenue cycle, so their compensation metrics must reflect what they can truly control and impact.

Before diving into role-by-role guidance, remember that compensation misalignment can quietly derail performance. When reps are measured on outcomes they don't control, motivation plummets and behavior skews. The following breakdown ensures each role's incentives reflect its true sphere of influence.

· **SDRs**: Pay on qualified pipeline created, so focus remains on generating quality opportunities rather than sheer activity volume. For example, a SaaS company that paid SDRs purely on meeting count found leads unqualified and AE conversion rates dropping. Shifting to pipeline value increased both SDR discipline and AE confidence.

· **AEs**: Pay on closed revenue, with accelerators for over-achievement, driving urgency and rewarding those who push beyond quota. One industrial distributor found that without accelerators, top reps capped out early and coasted. Adding accelerators lifted over-quota attainment by 20%.

· **AMs/CSMs**: Blend renewals, expansion, and NRR (net revenue retention), reinforcing the importance of protecting and growing the base. A tech firm that paid AMs only on renewals saw flat growth; introducing expansion metrics spurred upsell motions and lifted NRR.

· **Overlays/SEs**: Mix team-based measures and MBOs, ensuring collaboration across deals and rewarding contributions that don't show up directly as bookings but are essential to success. Without team-based credit, SEs chased visibility instead of supporting reps. Adding shared metrics improved win rates and deal velocity.

Pitfalls to Avoid

It's important to call out some of the most common pitfalls that derail even well-intentioned compensation plans. These are patterns observed across industries and company sizes, and they often stem from the tension between Finance, strategy, and sales execution. Recognizing them early can save both trust and performance:

· **Over-complicating plans with too many levers**. Reps should be able to explain their plan in a sentence; when complexity increases, motivation decreases.

· **Designing based on Finance goals, not market reality**. Compensation must reflect how deals are actually won and where opportunity exists, not just top-down budget expectations.

- **Ignoring pay equity across territories or segments**. If one rep has a structurally easier patch than another but identical targets and pay, you create distrust and churn.

- **Changing mid-year without clear communication**. Frequent or poorly explained changes erode credibility. If adjustments are necessary, tie them to transparent business shifts and provide clear rationale and examples.

Avoiding these pitfalls isn't just about preventing mistakes, it's about building credibility. When comp plans are clear, fair, and grounded in reality, they inspire confidence and unlock performance rather than resistance.

Governance and Communication

Before compensation plans go live, governance and communication determine whether they land with clarity or confusion. The right structures ensure alignment, transparency, and trust. This is where leadership demonstrates that compensation isn't a mysterious black box but a fair and transparent system that connects business goals to individual opportunity.

- Run an **annual compensation council** with Sales, RevOps, and Finance to ensure alignment with business priorities and market realities. This council should review attainment data, payout distribution, and feedback from the field to keep plans relevant and trusted.

- **Pilot new structures** with a small group before broad rollout, so potential issues surface early without disrupting the entire salesforce.

- **Provide reps with transparent calculators**, FAQs, and real-world examples, giving them confidence in how their performance ties to earnings.

- **Monitor payout vs. performance quarterly**, not just to track cost but to detect whether the plan is driving the intended behaviors. Share insights with leadership and adjust where misalignment appears.

Compensation plans succeed not just because of their design, but because of how they are communicated and governed. When governance is structured and communication transparent, the field gains confidence that leadership has their back, and motivation follows.

Analyzing Comp Plan Performance

Designing a plan is only half the battle. Measuring whether it works is what turns compensation from theory into practice. Analysis ensures incentives are driving the right outcomes, not just producing payouts.

Key dimensions to track include:

- **Attainment distribution:** Are most reps clustered around 90–110% of quota, or is performance polarized? Healthy plans show a balanced curve, not just a few stars carrying the team.

- **Payout vs. performance:** Are high earners truly your highest performers, or are loopholes creating misaligned rewards?

- **Cost of sales:** Is total compensation expense aligned with revenue growth and profitability targets?

- **Behavioral signals:** Are reps chasing small deals to hit volume targets, or focusing on strategic accounts as intended?

- **Retention and morale:** Do reps feel the plan is fair, transparent, and worth staying for? Exit interviews and engagement surveys provide leading indicators here.

Best practice: review comp plan performance quarterly, not just annually. Use both quantitative data (payout ratios, attainment spreads) and qualitative feedback (rep sentiment, manager insights) to refine the plan. Done well, analysis transforms compensation from a static contract into a continuous lever for alignment and growth.

Case Example: Diagnosing Plan Effectiveness

Consider a global industrial equipment company that noticed an odd trend: total revenue was rising, but profit margins were shrinking. Analysis of their comp plan revealed that reps were chasing small, quick-close deals because volume was over-weighted in the plan, while larger, more strategic deals were neglected. By shifting weight to deal size and multi-year contract value, the company reversed the trend within two quarters, profitability rose, and strategic accounts regained attention.

This underscores why analyzing comp plans is not optional. Without a feedback loop, incentives can easily drive unintended behavior.

Wrap-Up: Incentives as a Growth Engine

When strategy, quotas, and compensation align, behavior follows. Incentives become the connective tissue between GTM intent and human motivation. But alignment is only real if it is monitored. Comp plans must be analyzed continuously to ensure they are rewarding the right outcomes. Get this right, and execution gains both direction and energy; get it wrong, and even the best strategies stall.

In the next chapter, we'll close the GTM Planning pillar by exploring how to embed all of these elements into a **repeatable GTM planning cadence and operating rhythm**, ensuring planning is a living system rather than a one-time event.

Chapter 7: Operationalizing GTM Planning

"A strategy that can't be executed repeatedly is just a high-cost suggestion."

Even well-crafted GTM strategies fail when the planning process itself is disjointed, reactive, or overly theoretical. Annual planning becomes a once-a-year scramble to hit a number, with minimal alignment across functions and little continuity into execution. The result? Mismatched quotas, delayed hiring, unfunded priorities, and a sales force that's still ramping by the time Q2 hits.

Planning isn't a phase. It's a **system**. One that must be cross-functional, time-bound, and directly linked to how the business executes. This chapter is about building that system.

GTM Planning as a Closed Loop System

It's important to establish what makes great planning different: it's not a one-time event but a continuous system. Great planning operates as a closed loop that connects:

- **Strategy** (where and how to compete)

- **Design** (coverage, roles, comp, programs)

- **Execution readiness** (enablement, tools, content)

- **Performance feedback** (what's working, what's not)

Each stage must have clear owners, decision forums, timelines, and KPIs. The loop ensures that lessons from execution feed directly into the next round of planning, creating continuous improvement instead of annual reinvention. Monitoring this loop is critical: if compensation design, coverage models, or enablement aren't producing the intended outcomes, it will quickly show up in performance feedback. Organizations that ignore these signals end up repeating mistakes; those that monitor and act on them continuously refine their GTM engine and keep incentives, roles, and strategy aligned.

Planning Cadence: Annual, Quarterly, Ongoing

Before discussing cadence types, it's worth noting why cadence matters: without a rhythm, planning becomes episodic, disconnected, and reactive. A layered cadence keeps leadership and field aligned, turning planning into a continuous conversation instead of a yearly scramble.

Break the cycle of "set and forget" with a layered cadence:

Cycle	Focus	Key Outputs
Annual (Q3–Q4)	Strategic direction, segmentation, org design, headcount	GTM model, hiring plan, budget
Quarterly (pre-QBR)	Execution adjustments, program calibration, territory refinements	Resource shifts, sales play focus
Ongoing (monthly)	Signal monitoring: pipeline health, coverage issues, rep feedback	Input for agile iteration

This rhythm keeps strategy tethered to reality, long-term enough to steer the ship, frequent enough to course-correct. It creates a shared tempo across functions, anchoring conversations in evidence and milestones.

Best practice: link these cadences to revenue milestones, **not** arbitrary calendar dates. You're planning around performance, not just time.

Cadence is culture. The more predictable and trusted the rhythm, the easier it is for teams to engage, prepare, and act with confidence.

Cross-Functional Ownership

One of the biggest failures in GTM planning is lack of accountability. Without clear ownership, responsibilities blur, and strategic intent turns into finger-pointing when targets are missed. That's why cross-functional swim lanes must be explicit and consistently reinforced.

Define clear swim lanes:

· **Sales:** Define and own targets, hiring profiles, and segment-specific goals

· **RevOps:** Own the data model, tooling, and scenario planning

· **Finance:** Provide financial guardrails and validate assumptions

- **Enablement:** Scope onboarding and readiness needs tied to the plan

- **Marketing:** Align campaigns and demand generation plays

- **Product:** Feed in roadmap and packaging updates

Run a GTM planning council that brings these voices together regularly. No silos, no surprises. A well-run council doesn't just share updates; it makes decisions, resolves conflicts, and holds each function accountable.

Accountability in planning isn't about bureaucracy, it's about clarity. When every function knows its role and the council keeps them aligned, GTM planning becomes a driver of trust and execution rather than confusion and rework.

Tools and Infrastructure

Planning at scale can't run off disconnected spreadsheets. Without a unified system, silos emerge, assumptions drift, and leaders waste cycles reconciling different versions of the truth. A centralized planning workspace becomes the single source of alignment, allowing decisions to be made on facts, not fragments. Use a centralized planning workspace that integrates:

- Account segmentation and whitespace mapping

- Rep coverage and capacity models

- Quota modeling and performance projections

- Hiring ramp curves

- Scenario simulations (e.g., what happens if we hire 3 months late?)

Leverage platforms that connect to CRM and HRIS data, so plans aren't disconnected from real-world inputs.

Tools don't replace judgment, but they amplify it. The more connected your planning infrastructure, the faster you can test assumptions, course-correct, and keep GTM execution tethered to reality.

Execution Readiness Check

Before you finalize plans, it's critical to validate whether the organization is actually ready to execute against them. Too often, leaders assume alignment and only discover gaps once the quarter is underway. A structured readiness check acts as the final stress test of your GTM plan.

Key questions to ask:

· Do we have enough **pipeline** in the segments we're assigning, and is it at the right stage mix to support targets?

· Are new reps expected to **ramp fast enough**, given realistic onboarding capacity and territory potential?

· Are enablement programs and content **mapped** to segment needs and selling motions, not just generic training?

· Have frontline managers been **trained and briefed** on what's changing, why it matters, and how to coach to it?

Don't assume alignment, inspect it.

Readiness is where plans turn into reality. A few disciplined checks before launch can prevent quarters of misfires, ensuring execution starts sharp and focused.

Communication & Change Management

Rolling out the plan is as critical as designing it. Even the best strategy will collapse if people can't understand, believe in, or act on it. Communication and change management transform a static document into a shared playbook. Focus on:

· **Manager enablement:** Can they explain and reinforce the plan, translate it into day-to-day priorities, and coach their teams through change? Managers are the first translators of strategy, and their confidence shapes the field's confidence.

· **Sales kickoff narrative:** Is the story about "why we're doing this" clear, compelling, and tied to the company's broader strategy so that reps feel part of something bigger than their quota? A powerful kickoff frames the plan as a movement, not just a math exercise.

- **Field feedback loops:** Is there a reliable, two-way channel for real-world friction to be surfaced quickly, discussed openly, and acted upon so the plan evolves with reality rather than assumptions? Feedback is oxygen for credibility.

GTM plans don't fail because of spreadsheets, but because people don't understand them, believe in them, or know how to act on them. Treat communication and change management as the final mile of planning, and you ensure the plan doesn't just exist, it lives.

Wrap-Up: Planning is a Competitive Advantage

Companies that embrace GTM planning as a living operating system -not a disconnected annual exercise- move faster, adapt quicker, and execute with precision. They link effort to opportunity and resources to results, while creating confidence and clarity across the field. The discipline of monitoring, adjusting, and communicating turns planning into a continuous source of competitive advantage rather than a once-a-year ritual.

With planning in place, we now shift to the next pillar: **Sales Execution**. This is where strategy comes alive in pipeline creation, deal progression, coaching moments, and customer conversations. It is the proving ground where the intent of planning is stress-tested by the reality of the market.

Part II: Sales Execution

Chapter 8: Sales Process as Competitive Advantage

"Great sellers can win deals. Great sales processes build repeatable revenue."

In too many companies, the sales process is either nonexistent, theoretical, or ignored. It lives in a slide deck from Sales Enablement or buried in CRM stage definitions that no one follows. Reps treat it like optional guidance. Managers inspect deals based on gut feel. Leadership complains about inconsistent execution but lacks a system to enforce it.

A strong sales process is more than a flowchart. It's a blueprint for how your organization consistently turns opportunities into wins. It includes buyer-aligned stages, objective exit criteria, required activities, and clear role ownership. The goal is design, not documentation, because a well-designed process is a living asset that adapts with your market and products.

Defining a Real Sales Process

Let's be clear: a real sales process is not the same as your CRM stages.

At each stage, think beyond your sales motion: What decision is the buyer making? What evidence will build their confidence to move forward? What objections are likely to surface? And what role do we play in shaping their decision? A buyer-centric process maps your internal steps to the customer's journey, ensuring you're not just pushing deals forward; you're helping buyers make good decisions quickly.

A complete sales process includes:

- **Defined stages** that align to buyer behavior, not just internal tasks, ensuring the process mirrors how customers actually make decisions rather than internal checklists.

- **Exit criteria** for each stage -objective, testable, and enforced- to create clarity and eliminate subjectivity when moving opportunities forward.

- **Activities** required to advance (e.g., discovery complete, value confirmed) that make it clear what must be accomplished in each stage, leaving no room for skipping critical steps.

- **Roles involved** (who owns what step/ activity: AE, SE, SDR, AM) to drive accountability and collaboration across the revenue team.

- **Tools used** (CRM, call recording, ROI calculators, proposal software) that support activities and embed the process into daily workflows, making it measurable, repeatable, and easier to follow.

This isn't documentation, it's design. The more rigor you apply here, the more predictability you'll get downstream.

Buyer-Centric Process Design

The process must map to how your buyers buy, not how you want to sell. For each stage, you should step into the buyer's world and ask:

- What decision is the buyer making at this point?

- What evidence do they need to feel confident?

- What objections are likely to surface?

- What role does sales need to play to help them advance?

It's not enough to just define stages; you must understand the psychology of the buyer. Each stage represents a distinct decision moment. For example, consensus-building among internal stakeholders may require new content, executive engagement, or a business case the champion can socialize. If that's what the buyer needs, then it must be part of your process, not a step you hope happens organically.

Consider also the tools that support each buyer milestone: ROI calculators, customer reference libraries, call recordings for coaching, and executive decks. These aren't just enablers; they are proof points that help buyers justify their decision and reduce friction.

Example: If your buyer needs to build internal consensus before shortlisting vendors, that's not a stage to skip. It's a job your rep needs to guide with the right activities, collateral, and coaching support. Done well, this prevents deals from stalling at "90%" and accelerates movement toward a confident decision.

Qualification Frameworks that Matter

A sales process without strong qualification is just pipeline decoration.

Popular models like MEDDPICC, BANT, and SPIN still work, but only when reps and managers apply them with discipline. These frameworks provide a common language for evaluating opportunities, but they only deliver value if applied consistently and tied to real business outcomes.

Strong organizations:

- Integrate qualification into **stage gates** so that deals cannot progress without meeting minimum standards

- Train managers to **coach on it**, not just ask for it, embedding qualification into deal reviews and forecast calls

- Align **forecast categories** to qualification status, so reporting reflects reality rather than optimism

- Use qualification as a **deal scoring mechanism** to prioritize resources, not just a checklist

Think of qualification as a **risk filter**. It should actively shape where reps spend time, focusing attention on opportunities that are both winnable and worth winning. By doing so, teams avoid the trap of bloated pipelines filled with low probability deals, and instead concentrate their energy on the opportunities most likely to deliver impact.

Standardizing Across Segments and Motions

You don't need a single monolithic sales process. But you do need consistency and clarity across your GTM motions.

Consistency drives scalability. Core process stages and definitions should be standardized across the company, while allowing segment-specific variations in thresholds, roles, and cycle expectations. Without this balance, you either end up with rigidity that doesn't fit all segments, or chaos where every rep invents their own approach.

Think of it this way: your sales process is your operating language. If every rep speaks a different dialect, you cannot measure, forecast, or coach effectively. But if everyone speaks the same base language, with room for local accents (Enterprise vs. SMB, new logo vs. expansion), then both reporting and execution become scalable.

Segment-specific processes (e.g., Enterprise vs. SMB) should:

· Share a **core structure** anchored in buyer-aligned stages

· Tailor **deal size thresholds, sales roles, and expected cycle lengths** to reflect reality in each motion

· Be **clearly understood** across teams so that leadership, RevOps, and Enablement know how to support each segment

Avoid the trap of "every rep does it their way." That doesn't scale, doesn't forecast, and ultimately undermines credibility with leadership and investors.

Manager Accountability and Enforcement

Your sales process is only as strong as your **frontline managers** make it. Sales managers are the guardians of process discipline. They are the ones who translate methodology into daily execution, ensuring that the rigor designed into the process is lived out in every deal review, coaching session, and forecast call.

Enforce discipline through:

· **Stage-based inspection**: Don't advance a deal unless exit criteria are met. Managers must hold the line here, reinforcing that shortcuts today become misses tomorrow.

· **Deal reviews**: Rooted in process, not personality. Reviews should test whether opportunities meet the defined criteria and whether the rep has truly advanced the buyer's decision-making.

· **Coaching**: Focused on opportunity strategy within process boundaries, helping reps think critically rather than simply pushing them for numbers.

Strong managers make the process real by consistently modeling behaviors, using the process as their own management framework, and holding reps accountable for living up to it. Without this, even the best-designed process collapses into subjectivity and noise. If managers aren't fluent in the process, data integrity falls apart, coaching loses its anchor, and the process itself becomes irrelevant.

Embedding the Process in Systems

Your process must live where the work happens. Operationalize the process in your tools so it's not an abstract framework but a tangible guide for daily execution:

- **CRM**: Stage definitions, required fields, automated alerts, and embedded guidance that nudge reps toward best practice.

- **Call recording**: Tag calls to key process stages for analysis, coaching, and pattern recognition across teams.

- **Sales and CS playbooks**: Contextual content and actions embedded directly in workflows, providing just-in-time support that maps to the buyer journey.

- **Dashboards**: Visualize progression rates, stuck deals, and conversion metrics, while also linking performance to leading indicators like activity quality or multi-threading depth.

- **Enablement and knowledge platforms**: Integrate training, certifications, and content libraries so that reps can access learning at the moment of need.

When the process is embedded in the daily flow of work, it stops being perceived as overhead. Instead, it becomes second nature, shaping rep behavior automatically and allowing managers to focus their coaching on strategy and quality rather than mechanics. Over time, this creates a culture where process discipline and data integrity reinforce one another, turning systems into true accelerators of performance.

Putting It All Together

End-to-end GTM motions aren't linear, they form a continuum, best represented as a flywheel or an infinity loop (see figure below for an example). The close of a sale is not the end, but the handoff into customer success and retention. When executed well, this creates a continuous loop where adoption, value realization, and satisfaction naturally lead to renewals, cross-sell, and upsell opportunities. In other words, every deal won is the starting line for the next opportunity.

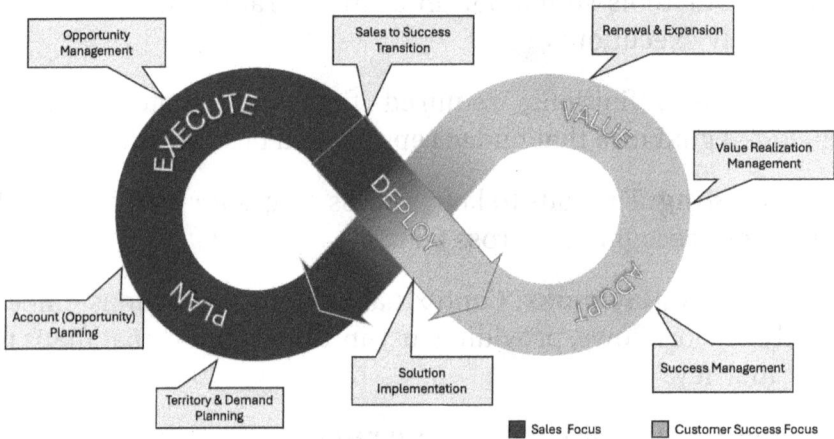

For clarity purposes, the linear representation of sales and customer success processes can be broken down into activities, exit criteria, roles involved, and tools to be used across.

Here's a generic example of a **Buyer-Centric Sales Process**:

Element / Stage	Discovery & Qualification	Solution Validation	Business Case & Consensus	Negotiation & Close
Activities	Discovery call, stakeholder mapping, pain confirmation	Demo, proof-of-concept, technical validation	ROI analysis, case study sharing, and executive alignment	Proposal review, pricing discussions, legal & procurement
Exit Criteria	Budget, authority, need, timeline validated	Technical fit confirmed, champion identified	Economic buyer aligned, business case accepted	Signed agreement, implementation plan agreed
Roles Involved	SDR, AE	AE, SE, Product Specialist	AE, SE, Exec Sponsor, Finance	AE, Legal, Exec Sponsor
Tools Used	CRM, call recording, discovery templates	Demo environment, battlecards, ROI calculator	Mutual Action Plan, value calculators, executive decks	Proposal software, contract management system, e-signature

This illustrates how activities, criteria, roles, and tools map across buyer-aligned stages. To truly close the loop, best-in-class organizations extend the process beyond Close into **Customer Success and Retention** stages:

Element / Stage	Implement & Onboarding	Adoption & Value Realization	Renewal & Expansion	Advocacy & Retention
Activities	Kickoff, success planning, training sessions	Usage monitoring, QBRs, value delivery reviews	Renewal discussions, upsell/cross-sell plays	Reference calls, case studies, and customer council participation
Exit Criteria	Customer is live on the solution, success plan agreed	Usage goals met, Measurable value delivered	Renewal secured, expansion committed	Customer actively advocates, participates in programs
Roles Involved	CSM, Implementation Specialist, AE	CSM, Support, Product Specialist	CSM, AE, Finance, Exec Sponsor	CSM, Marketing, Exec Sponsor
Tools Used	Onboarding portal, project management software	Analytics dashboards, survey tools	Renewal playbooks, CPQ, CRM	Advocacy platforms, community portals, referral tools

Wrap-Up: Discipline Creates Freedom

Reps often resist process, thinking it slows them down. In reality, a good process does the opposite: it eliminates wasted effort, sharpens focus, and improves coaching. It becomes the backbone of GTM execution.

In the next chapter, we'll dig into **Lead Generation**, because before you can manage opportunities, you need a predictable engine for creating them. The quality of your pipeline begins with how effectively you generate, capture, and qualify demand.

Chapter 9: Lead Generation - Fueling the Pipeline Engine

"Pipeline doesn't just happen. It's generated by design, not by chance."

Lead generation is often misunderstood as a narrow Marketing exercise, when in fact it is the lifeblood of the entire GTM system. This chapter examines how organizations move from market definitions and ICP clarity into the execution of programs that produce real opportunities. It explores how inbound, outbound, partner, and account-based motions can be orchestrated into a balanced pipeline engine, how clear definitions and rigorous metrics prevent wasted effort, and how technology and AI are reshaping what is possible. At its core, lead generation is positioned here not as a tactical campaign activity, but as a strategic growth lever that links planning to execution and powers the forecasting engine.

Why Lead Generation Matters

Without consistent top-of-funnel activity, even the best sales process runs dry. Pipeline is the *lifeblood* of GTM execution, and lead generation is how it is produced at scale. It aligns Sales and Marketing to a common purpose: creating qualified opportunities, and it serves as the critical bridge between planning -defining markets and ICPs- and execution, where pipeline is managed and deals are closed. Without a deliberate lead generation strategy, even the sharpest coverage model or sales process framework collapses under the weight of an empty funnel.

Lead generation is also a *signal generator*: the health of your funnel reflects whether ICP definitions, messaging, and coverage strategies are resonating in the real world. For growing companies, it is the lever that moves GTM efforts from theory to traction. Without it, execution becomes an exercise in managing scarcity rather than scaling opportunity. In short, lead generation is not just an entry point. It is the proof point that planning was correct and the foundation upon which forecasting can be built.

It also serves as a cultural forcing function. Organizations that prioritize disciplined lead generation naturally embed data-driven decision-making and cross-functional accountability into their DNA. At scale, this discipline separates companies that merely "hunt for deals" from those that consistently **design demand**. The former live quarter-to-quarter; the latter create a compounding pipeline engine that drives sustainable growth.

Foundations: From ICP to Campaigns

Lead generation begins with a clear blueprint. TAM, SAM, SOM, ICP, and personas (covered earlier in Part I) become the practical foundation for demand programs. Translating planning into execution requires sharpening messaging around the pain points and priorities of each persona, while ensuring coverage models define the balance between outbound and inbound motions. In this context, quality matters more than volume. A smaller number of highly qualified leads will consistently outperform a flood of unfiltered names. Campaigns anchored in ICP clarity and persona relevance not only yield higher conversions but also accelerate sales cycles by putting sellers in front of buyers who are already primed for engagement.

Lead generation succeeds when campaigns are tightly mapped to strategy, not when they chase numbers for their own sake. When companies design demand programs in alignment with the broader GTM plan, they ensure that every dollar spent and every hour invested contributes to building meaningful pipeline. This alignment transforms campaigns from tactical exercises into strategic growth levers. It also provides a feedback loop: if the market does not respond, the issue often lies upstream in ICP definition or value proposition clarity. In this way, lead generation is both the execution engine and the early warning system of GTM strategy.

Lead Generation Channels

Lead generation is not a one-size-fits-all exercise. Every company must design its channel mix based on its ICP, deal size, and sales motion. In SaaS, inbound digital demand often drives scale. In industrial sectors, outbound and partner ecosystems still carry disproportionate weight.

What matters is building a balanced portfolio that generates a predictable flow of qualified opportunities.

Think of channels as investment buckets. Some create *volume* (lots of names, lower quality), others create *precision* (fewer names, higher conversion). The art of GTM execution is blending these channels to match your growth strategy.

Comparison of Lead Generation Channels

Channel	Typical Tactics	Cost per Lead	Scalability	Conversion Quality	Best Fit For
Inbound	Content Marketing, SEO, paid search, webinars, PLG free trials	Low–Medium	High	Medium (varies by targeting)	SaaS & tech with strong digital reach
Outbound	SDR cold calls/emails, intent-driven outreach, trade shows/events	Medium–High	Medium	High (if ICP-focused)	Enterprise & industrial with defined target accounts
Partner / Ecosystem	Co-Marketing, resellers, referral programs, marketplaces	Medium	Medium–High	High (trusted by buyers)	Complex solutions, ecosystems, and industrial
Hybrid / ABM	1:1 account personalization, targeted campaigns, multi-channel orchestration	High	Low–Medium	Very High	Strategic accounts, big enterprise deals

Framing this mix as a portfolio strategy reinforces the idea that over-reliance on a single channel creates vulnerability, while diversification builds resilience.

Inbound shines when buyers are digitally active and research-driven. A strong content engine builds awareness and trust, but inbound alone often floods the funnel with unqualified names if ICP filters aren't tight. Outbound, by contrast, remains one of the most controllable levers. When targeted against the right accounts, SDRs can open doors competitors miss. In industrial markets, outbound often means boots-on-the-ground prospecting and event networking. Partner and ecosystem leads usually arrive with higher intent, because they come through a trusted channel, though the challenge lies in aligning incentives and attribution. Hybrid or ABM approaches are the most resource-intensive but also the most effective for high-value pursuits, delivering highly personalized engagement that significantly raises win rates.

Stage of company matters: early-stage SaaS often leans inbound for scale, mature enterprises develop outbound and ABM muscle for strategic penetration, and industrial companies continue to depend heavily on channel partners and events.

Defining and Qualifying Leads

One of the most common breakdowns between Marketing and Sales isn't *volume of leads*, it's *clarity of definition*. Marketing celebrates "10,000 new leads this quarter," while Sales complains, "None of them are qualified." Both are right, because without shared criteria, "lead" means very different things.

Defining and qualifying leads is therefore foundational to GTM execution. Clear definitions ensure that Marketing optimizes campaigns toward outcomes Sales actually values, that Sales trusts and engages the leads it receives, and that RevOps can measure conversion at every handoff without ambiguity. The three standard stages of lead qualification -MQL, SAL, and SQL- provide the common language, but each company must customize the details to its ICP, sales cycle, and deal size.

Lead Qualification Stages

Stage	Definition	Ownership	Exit Criteria
MQL (Marketing Qualified Lead)	A lead that fits ICP basics (company size, industry, persona) and has engaged with content/campaigns	Marketing	Meets scoring threshold (downloads, clicks, event attendance)
SAL (Sales Accepted Lead)	A lead passed from Marketing that Sales has reviewed and agreed is worth pursuing	Shared (Sales + Mktg)	Explicit acceptance by SDR/rep; lead not rejected for bad fit
SQL (Sales Qualified Lead)	A lead that has been directly engaged by Sales and validated as an active opportunity	Sales	Confirmed need, budget, authority, or timeline (based on BANT, MEDDICC, or other qualification)

MQLs are the broadest stage, signaling *interest* but not necessarily *intent*. The danger is flooding Sales with too many that don't convert. SALs represent the handshake between Marketing and Sales, a step often skipped but crucial to prevent junk leads from passing downstream and to create accountability. SQLs are where Sales takes full ownership: the point where the lead has been validated as a real opportunity. When these definitions are codified and agreed upon, pipeline reviews shift from finger-pointing to problem-solving, with focus placed on improving conversion rates between stages.

Case Example: The Cost of Ambiguity: At one SaaS company, Marketing delivered 5,000 MQLs per quarter, but only 5% became opportunities. Sales leaders dismissed Marketing's value. After redefining SAL and instituting a two-day SLA for reps to accept or reject leads, conversions doubled to 10%. The difference wasn't more leads, it was clearer definitions and accountability at the handoff.

Metrics That Matter in Lead Generation

Lead generation is notorious for producing *vanity metrics* such as clicks, impressions, or downloads. These show activity, but they don't prove impact. To elevate lead generation into a true business driver, GTM teams must track metrics that link top-of-funnel activity directly to pipeline and revenue outcomes. The right metrics provide two critical views: leading indicators that forecast future pipeline health, and lagging indicators that validate whether past efforts created real business impact.

Lead Generation Metrics Framework

Category	Metric	Type	Why It Matters
Volume	Number of leads generated (by channel, by campaign)	Leading	Gauges initial reach and campaign effectiveness.
Quality	% of MQLs accepted as SALs	Leading	Indicates alignment between Marketing and Sales; filters noise early.
Velocity	Average time from lead → SAL → SQL	Leading	Measures how quickly leads progress, a proxy for intent and process efficiency.
Conversion	Lead-to-opportunity conversion rate (MQL → SQL)	Lagging	Shows the *true yield* of lead generation efforts.
Pipeline Impact	$ pipeline created per campaign/channel	Lagging	Connects lead gen directly to opportunity creation.
Revenue Impact	% of closed-won deals sourced by channel	Lagging	Validates which lead sources actually drive revenue, not just activity.
ROI	Cost per lead / Cost per opportunity	Lagging	Ensures resources are allocated to channels that produce profitable returns.

Volume tells you if the engine is running, but without quality it creates waste. *Quality* metrics, such as *MQL-to-SAL acceptance* rates, are especially powerful for uncovering Marketing–Sales misalignment. *Velocity* is an important leading signal of intent, since true buyers move quickly while tire-kickers stall. *Conversion* rates reveal whether leads are translating into opportunities or just filling dashboards. *Pipeline* and *revenue impact* demonstrate that lead generation is a growth driver rather than a cost center. And *ROI* forces discipline, ensuring resources chase outcomes rather than vanity numbers.

Example: An industrial company relied heavily on trade shows, producing thousands of scanned badges. Only 2% converted into opportunities, at a cost per lead four times higher than digital inbound. By shifting 30% of budget to inbound content campaigns, they doubled SQLs without increasing spend. The difference came from measuring conversion and ROI rather than volume alone.

Role of Technology and AI in Lead Generation

Technology has always shaped how leads are generated -think of the evolution from business cards at trade shows, to email automation, to today's intent data platforms-. With the rise of AI, lead generation is undergoing a more fundamental shift: from manual list-building and broad outreach to predictive, personalized, and scalable engagement.

Here's the new reality: anyone can send an email, build a landing page, or scrape a prospect list. What now differentiates is the precision, personalization, and orchestration of those efforts.

How Technology and AI Transform Lead Generation

Capability	What It Does	Impact
AI-Powered Prospecting	Uses intent data, buying signals, and firmographics to surface best-fit accounts	Reps focus on "in-market" buyers, not cold lists
Predictive Lead Scoring	Applies ML models to rank leads by likelihood to convert	Increases sales productivity by prioritizing high-potential leads
GenAI Personalization	Automates tailored emails, call scripts, and landing pages at scale	Balances efficiency with 1:1 relevance
Conversational AI	Chatbots and digital assistants that qualify leads in real time	Accelerates velocity and creates 24/7 coverage

| **Marketing Automation Platforms** | Orchestrate nurture journeys across channels (email, social, ads) | Keeps prospects engaged until sales-ready |
| **Data Enrichment Tools** | Append firmographic and technographic data to raw leads | Improves quality and targeting accuracy |

AI-powered prospecting flips the model: instead of sellers asking "Who should I call today?", the system suggests "Here are the accounts most likely to be buying." Predictive lead scoring removes guesswork from prioritization, helping reps focus on meaningful signals rather than noise. GenAI personalization blends efficiency with relevance, allowing one SDR to send fifty personalized notes in the time it once took to write five. Conversational AI extends coverage, capturing qualification data in real time and feeding it directly into CRM systems. And data enrichment ensures Marketing and Sales are working with complete, accurate profiles.

But technology does not replace the human element, it amplifies it. AI can surface the *what* and *when*, but humans must still provide the *why*. Sellers need context, strategic insight, and empathy, capabilities machines cannot replicate.

Callout: The Double-Edged Sword of AI in Lead Gen: The upside is faster, smarter targeting and personalization at scale. The risk is over-automation that erodes trust and floods prospects with noise. The balance is using AI to augment sellers, not replace them. The differentiator becomes judgment, not activity.

Sales and Marketing Alignment

If lead generation is the engine, then Sales and Marketing alignment is the fuel. Without it, the engine sputters; Marketing celebrates campaign clicks, Sales dismisses the leads, and pipeline stalls. Alignment is not about being friendly; it is about shared definitions, accountability, and feedback loops that make the system work.

Common breakdowns include Marketing's perspective that "we delivered thousands of leads, but Sales isn't following up," and Sales' counterpoint that "these aren't real leads; they don't fit our ICP or buying cycle." The truth is that both sides are working hard, but without shared goals and criteria, effort is wasted.

What Good Looks Like

Alignment Mechanism	What It Looks Like	Impact
Shared Pipeline Targets	Marketing and Sales commit to jointly sourced pipeline goals, not separate metrics.	Eliminates finger-pointing; fosters joint accountability.
Lead Definitions & SLAs	Clear MQL → SAL → SQL criteria, plus agreed timelines for follow-up (e.g., 48 hours).	Creates trust in handoffs; prevents lead leakage.
Feedback Loops	Regular reviews of lead quality and conversion data, with Sales input into campaigns.	Ensures continuous improvement; stops wasting budget.
Joint Planning	Marketing and Sales co-design campaign calendars, events, and ABM plays.	Aligns message, timing, and coverage to maximize impact.
RevOps as Orchestrator	Neutral function ensures data accuracy, definitions, and process governance.	Keeps alignment durable beyond individual leaders' tenure.

Shared pipeline targets are a game-changer: instead of Marketing optimizing for volume and Sales for conversion, both are measured on contribution to qualified pipeline. SLAs bring discipline, requiring Marketing to deliver leads that meet agreed criteria and Sales to follow up promptly. Feedback loops matter because markets evolve, and regular joint reviews allow real-time course correction. RevOps plays the role of referee and translator, owning definitions, data, and reporting to ensure alignment is durable rather than dependent on personalities.

Example: At a mid-market SaaS company, Marketing generated thousands of MQLs per quarter, but Sales claimed only 10% were worth pursuing. By instituting a 24-hour SLA for reps to accept or reject leads, plus bi-weekly feedback reviews, the company doubled acceptance rates and increased pipeline contribution from Marketing by 35% within two quarters.

Wrap-Up: Pipeline as a System, Not a Surprise

Leads don't magically appear, and pipeline isn't built by chance. It is the outcome of a system; one where ICP clarity, disciplined channels, tight definitions, and strong Sales–Marketing alignment combine to fuel predictable growth. When lead generation is intentional, it builds confidence in the GTM engine. When it is haphazard, it leads to wasted effort, finger-pointing, and an empty forecast.

Key takeaways from this chapter include:

· **Clarity matters**: agreed definitions of MQL, SAL, and SQL prevent wasted motion.

· **Consistency scales**: disciplined, repeatable plays across inbound, outbound, partner, and ABM channels build resilience.

· **Collaboration sustains:** alignment between Sales and Marketing is essential for leads to become opportunities.

· **AI raises the bar**: technology enables targeting and personalization at scale, but human judgment remains the differentiator.

Lead generation is the lifeblood of GTM execution, the bridge between planning and pipeline. However, generating opportunities is only half the battle. The next step is ensuring those opportunities are managed with discipline, advanced with rigor, and forecasted with accuracy; a transition into the realm of pipeline management and forecasting, which forms the focus of the next chapters.

Chapter 10: Pipeline Management

"Your pipeline is not a spreadsheet. It's the heartbeat of your business."

Ask any CRO what keeps them up at night, and the answer is almost always some version of: *"I'm not confident in the pipeline."* It's either not big enough, not real enough, not moving fast enough, or all of the above.

Pipeline isn't just a forecasting tool. It's a **strategic asset**. It tells you if your GTM strategy is converting. If your sales process is working. If your reps are spending time in the right places. Managing it well is what separates high-performing organizations from high-anxiety ones.

Defining a Healthy Pipeline

Forget "more is better." Volume alone doesn't create confidence; **quality** and **velocity** matter more.

A healthy pipeline has the right **coverage, quality, and flow** to give leaders confidence and reps clarity:

- **Sufficient coverage**: Typically, 3-4x target, and dependent on your teams' win-rates adjusted for segment and cycle. Coverage is not about raw volume, but about ensuring there are enough well-qualified opportunities to hit quota.

- **Balanced aging**: Deals are distributed across stages without dangerous concentration at the very start or very end of the cycle. Balanced aging prevents the end-of-quarter scramble that exhausts reps and erodes customer trust.

- **Strong progression rates**: Opportunities are advancing steadily. Stalled deals are identified, addressed, or removed so that pipeline health reflects real momentum.

- **Clean data**: CRM hygiene is enforced. No ghost deals, no wishful close dates, and no unqualified fluff inflating numbers. Data integrity is what makes the pipeline a management tool rather than a false comfort.

A healthy pipeline also includes **clear visibility** into leading indicators: new opportunities created, early-stage conversions, and stage-to-stage progression. Leaders should be able to diagnose whether coverage is being replenished, velocity is improving, and quality is strengthening.

Healthy pipeline equals confidence in execution. It's not just a number on a dashboard... It's the heartbeat of your GTM system, and when it's managed well, it gives foresight, focus, and fuel for growth.

Coverage: One Metric, Many Mistakes

Most organizations use coverage ratio (pipeline ÷ quota) as a primary health indicator. But many get it wrong by:

- **Using a stale or padded pipeline** that inflates apparent health but masks risk.

- **Ignoring deal aging and segment mix**, which can distort the reality of conversion potential.

- **Over-relying on top-of-funnel MQLs or handoffs** without validating quality or conversion likelihood.

Fix it by:

- Defining **coverage by forecast period** (e.g., 90-day pipeline for 90-day target), so your ratio matches the time horizon you're managing.

- Setting **coverage expectations by segment** (Enterprise ≠ SMB). Use historical win-rates and cycle lengths to shape realistic expectations per segment, rather than applying a blanket multiplier.

- **Auditing pipeline quality weekly**, not just at EOQ. Leaders should run hygiene checks to ensure close dates are realistic, exit criteria are met, and opportunities haven't gone stale.

- Connecting coverage metrics to **velocity** and **win rates**. Coverage without movement or quality is just noise.

Coverage is a **directional signal**, a way to highlight potential gaps or surpluses. It should trigger inspection and action, not create a false sense of security. When combined with velocity and data integrity, it becomes a powerful early-warning system for revenue health.

Velocity: Moving Deals Through the Funnel

$$\textit{Pipeline Velocity} = \frac{(\textit{number of opportunities}) \times (\textit{average deal size}) \times (\textit{win rate})}{(\textit{sales cycle length})}$$

Velocity is a composite measure that captures the true **throughput of your pipeline**, how effectively raw opportunity is converted into revenue over time. High-performing teams treat velocity not just as math, but as a diagnostic lens to uncover bottlenecks.

High-performing teams manage **each lever**:

- **Create more quality opportunities** → via prospecting, ABM, channel programs, and targeted campaigns that align to the ICP.

- **Improve win rate** → via disciplined qualification, competitive plays, better discovery, and aligned proof points.

- **Shorten sales cycle** → via buyer enablement, clear mutual action plans, executive sponsorship, and urgency drivers.

- **Increase deal size** → via value selling, multi-threading, bundling, expansion into adjacent use cases, and executive engagement.

Advanced organizations go further by instrumenting velocity dashboards that allow leaders to isolate where drag is occurring. For example, if deal size is rising but win rate is falling, the problem may be poor qualification at the top of funnel. If opportunities are plentiful but sales cycles keep lengthening, the culprit may be lack of buyer enablement or poor deal orchestration.

Don't just measure pipeline, **diagnose it**. Break down each lever, run scenario analysis, and equip managers to coach reps on where to focus. Understanding what's dragging velocity and fixing it at the source turns the pipeline from a static metric into a dynamic management system.

Deal Hygiene and Stuck Opportunity Management

Pipeline decay is real. Deals that sit too long rot. Reps often leave them open out of hope, clinging to the possibility that something might happen. Managers sometimes avoid confronting these deals to sidestep friction with their teams. But this avoidance creates a false sense of security and clogs the funnel with dead weight.

The truth is that deals have a natural half-life. Without progress, energy, and buyer engagement, they decline in quality every day they linger. A pipeline filled with stale opportunities drains focus away from the real deals that can close.

To fight decay, establish hygiene rules and enforce them relentlessly:

- **Stage-specific aging thresholds** (e.g., no more than 30 days in stage 2 without advancement).

- **Mandatory next steps and close dates** for all deals, ensuring that every opportunity has a forward path.

- **Auto-expiry or review triggers** for idle opportunities, forcing managers and reps to make a conscious decision: advance it or clear it out.

- **Regular pipeline scrubs** as part of forecast meetings, where leaders actively challenge whether deals are real.

Advanced teams go further by using CRM alerts, AI-driven nudges, and manager dashboards to surface aging risks in real time. This turns hygiene into a proactive management tool rather than a quarterly cleanup exercise.

Healthy pipeline is **active pipeline**, filled with opportunities that are moving, current, and credible. Anything else is noise, distraction, and false comfort.

Pipeline Reviews: Coaching vs. Policing

Pipeline reviews should be more than inspection, they should be coaching moments where managers and reps jointly diagnose opportunities, sharpen strategy, and reinforce process discipline.

Too many managers use pipeline reviews as interrogation sessions. That creates defensive reps, bad data, and a culture where information is hidden rather than shared. Reviews should be collaborative working sessions that create clarity and confidence.

Instead:

· Review **early-stage** pipeline for top-of-funnel health: are we sourcing the right opportunities, aligned to ICP, with clear qualification?

· Use **mid-stage** reviews to coach on deal strategy: are reps multi-threading, building value, addressing risks, and aligning with buyer priorities?

· Inspect **late-stage** deals for forecast confidence: are exit criteria truly met, do we have a clear path to close, and what is the mitigation plan for risks?

Use a consistent question set to keep reviews focused and valuable:

· What's changed since last week?

· What's your next step and timeline?

· What risks do you see?

· What support do you need?

The goal isn't to catch reps off guard, but to make them better. Reviews should leave reps with clearer priorities, stronger strategies, and confidence in their pipeline. Done well, they become one of the most powerful development and forecasting tools in the sales manager's toolkit.

Dashboards That Matter

You don't need more dashboards. You need **better ones** that highlight the signal from the noise and make it actionable:

· **Pipeline by stage and age**, so you see both balance and bottlenecks

· **Coverage by segment and rep**, tied to quota and historic win-rates

- **Conversion rates by source and stage**, which show the efficiency of Marketing and Sales handoffs

- **Velocity benchmarks vs. actuals**, providing an early indicator of whether deals are moving at the pace needed

But dashboards shouldn't just show numbers. They should answer questions: Why is conversion dipping in one segment? Which reps consistently outperform benchmarks? Where is Marketing generating quality vs. noise?

Dashboards also serve as a unifying language across GTM.

Pro tip: Share pipeline snapshots regularly with Marketing, Customer Success, and Product. When everyone sees the same truth, debate shifts from data disputes to problem-solving. It's not just a sales asset, it's a **GTM signal**, a way of aligning the entire revenue engine around one shared reality.

Wrap-Up: Pipeline is Your Early Warning System

When managed right, your pipeline tells you what's coming, where to invest, and what to fix. It gives leadership foresight and reps focus. It's not just a report, it's a source of truth.

In the next chapter, we'll tackle **Forecasting Excellence**, because a strong pipeline is only useful if you can call the number with precision and accountability.

Chapter 11: Forecasting Excellence

"Hope is not a forecast. Precision is a leadership discipline."

Most sales forecasts are part art, part fiction. Reps sandbag or guess. Managers hedge or inflate. Leaders chase accuracy, but behind the curtain, it's often built on a mix of gut feel, outdated CRM entries, and last-minute spreadsheets.

But forecasting doesn't have to be a guessing game. When done right, it becomes a **core leadership system**, a way to drive accountability, align execution, and steer the business with confidence.

Forecasting is one of the clearest reflections of an organization's operational maturity. It's where market reality meets leadership judgment, and where credibility with the board and investors is either earned or lost.

This chapter is about turning forecasting from a rearview report into a forward-looking control mechanism.

Why Forecast Accuracy Isn't Optional Anymore

Forecasting used to be a QBR talking point. Now, it's a core GTM control system. Here's why:

1. Revenue predictability is the operating system of growth.

If you can't trust your forecast, you can't plan hiring, pipeline coverage, or working capital needs. Forecast accuracy creates enterprise confidence.

2. Investors and boards expect precision.

Missing the number once gets you a conversation. Missing it again costs you credibility. And in today's market, that can cost you funding or valuation.

3. It exposes execution health.

Forecasting isn't just about the numbers. It's a proxy for pipeline discipline, manager coaching, deal inspection, and rep performance.

When you operationalize forecasting, you're really operationalizing **go-to-market quality**.

Why Forecasts Break in Most Organizations

You don't need much experience to spot the usual culprits:

- **Forecast categories are loosely defined** (What does "commit" actually mean, and who decides?)

- **CRM hygiene is poor** (Stages are skipped, opps are inflated, key data is missing)

- **Roll-ups are subjective and last-minute** (Numbers shift wildly week to week, driven by pressure, not facts)

- **Reps and managers play it safe or political** (Sandbag to protect themselves, inflate to please leadership)

- **Tech is underutilized** (AI scores ignored, forecast modules unused, reporting fragmented)

Bottom line: most forecasts fail because there's **no consistent, inspectable process**.

What Forecasting Is (and Isn't)

Forecasting **IS NOT**:

- A summary of **what's in CRM**

- A **"rep roll-up"** exercise

- A weekly **fire drill**

Forecasting **IS**:

- A **disciplined, data-informed prediction** of likely revenue

- A **management tool for exposing risk** and driving action

- A **reflection of sales process quality** and opportunity health

Forecasting should connect field-level reality to executive decision-making. It should not only tell you what's likely to close, but also **why** it's likely, **what assumptions it depends on**, and **what could derail it**. A strong forecast surfaces risk early, enables resource allocation, and gives leaders the confidence to act rather than react.

Forecasting Methodologies

There are three primary approaches, often used in combination:

Method	Pros	Cons
Rep Commit/Roll-Up	Closest to field insight	Prone to optimism/sandbagging
Stage-Based /Weighted	Systematic, scalable	Assumes stage = likelihood (often untrue)
Predictive /AI Models	Powerful trend analysis	Needs strong data hygiene and volume

The most accurate forecasts blend human judgment, process rigor, and machine intelligence, each compensating for the blind spots of the others.

Forecast Cadence and Call Structure

Forecasting is not a meeting, it's a **rhythm**. Think of it as the organizational heartbeat that keeps Sales, Finance, and leadership aligned. Without rhythm, the forecast becomes reactive guesswork; with rhythm, it becomes a proactive operating system for the business.

Set a consistent cadence:

- **Weekly reviews** with managers and reps: focused on deal inspection, risk identification, and coaching opportunities

- **Biweekly roll-ups** at regional/segment level: where managers calibrate assumptions, align resources, and pressure test consistency across teams

- **Monthly exec reviews** with Finance and RevOps: turning the forecast into a company-wide decision tool, not just a sales number

Standardize the call structure so every forecast conversation drives value:

- What's changed since last week?

- What's in commit vs. upside vs. pipeline?

- What's at risk, and what's the plan to close it?

- What coverage exists for next period?

Great forecast calls don't just report, they **problem-solve**. They surface blind spots, clarify assumptions, and mobilize resources to close gaps. Done well, they create a culture of transparency and accountability where leaders are never surprised at quarter-end.

Forecast Categories: Define Them, Enforce Them

Avoid vague definitions like "commit" or "best case" that vary by manager. Create standardized categories and treat them as non-negotiable parts of your operating language:

- **Commit**: High confidence, exit criteria met, scheduled close date. These are the deals leadership can plan the business around.

- **Best Case/Upside**: Active opportunities with a clear path and some risk. They are worth attention and resources but should not be assumed in the core plan.

- **Pipeline**: Real opportunities that are being worked but are not forecastable this period. This is your future coverage and should be monitored for progression.

- **Omitted**: Deals with quality concerns or that are no longer viable. Keeping them visible in CRM inflates numbers and undermines credibility.

Make it clear **what earns a deal into each category** and inspect consistently. Train managers to challenge reps when deals are mislabeled, and review definitions in forecast calls to ensure alignment. Over time, this creates forecast integrity, builds trust with leadership, and prevents the cultural drift that happens when each manager defines categories their own way.

Forecast Accuracy as a Leadership Metric

Forecast accuracy isn't just a RevOps KPI, it's a reflection of leadership rigor and credibility. Boards and investors measure leaders by their ability to call the number, not just explain why it was missed.

Track:

- **Call accuracy** by manager, segment, and region to see who consistently calls it right

- **Variance** (over/under) by week and month to identify patterns of optimism or sandbagging

- **Slipped deals and reasons** to understand systemic issues (e.g., poor qualification, slow legal cycles, weak champions)

- **Rep-level accuracy** to reveal coaching needs and potential gaming of the system

- **Forecast bias trends** across the org (are teams consistently overconfident or too conservative?)

Use this data to coach, not punish. Share accuracy trends openly in leadership meetings to create transparency. Celebrate accuracy as a leadership competency.

The goal is to build a **forecasting culture** where precision is valued and credibility is earned, rather than a fear-based environment where reps and managers manipulate numbers to avoid scrutiny.

Role of Technology and AI

The advent of advanced technology and AI has created a step-change in forecasting. No longer limited to static roll-ups or stage-based probabilities, modern platforms can analyze signals across communication, behavior, and market data to provide predictive insight and early warnings. This opens new opportunities for leaders to move from reactive guesswork to proactive control.

Forecasting tools and AI models can:

- Identify risk based on email/calendar signals, activity patterns, and buyer engagement levels

- Highlight stale or slipping deals, surfacing risks earlier than human inspection alone

- Recommend commit categories based on past patterns, conversion probabilities, and deal attributes

- Project outcomes from coverage and velocity trends, giving leaders scenario-based foresight rather than static reports

Advanced platforms now integrate with CRM, call intelligence, and even external market data to provide predictive insights. Some tools can flag deals where champions are inactive, executive engagement is missing, or buying groups aren't multi-threaded, all signals that traditional roll-ups miss.

But tools only help if the fundamentals are strong:

- **Reps** must update CRM consistently, so data reflects reality

- **Managers** must enforce hygiene, challenging bad data and rewarding disciplined inputs

- **GTM leaders** must actually use the insights to make resource decisions, not treat them as interesting dashboards

AI doesn't replace accountability, it amplifies it. The more disciplined the organization is with data hygiene and process, the more powerful and trustworthy AI-driven forecasting becomes. Without that foundation, even the smartest algorithms generate noise instead of insight.

Wrap-Up: Confidence Over Consensus

Forecasting excellence isn't about pleasing the board or covering yourself, it's about creating confidence rooted in evidence, discipline, and foresight.

A modern forecast blends human judgment, rigorous process, and AI-driven insight to give leaders clarity on what's coming, why it's coming, and what risks must be mitigated. Done right, it becomes both a leadership tool and a cultural standard, translating execution into action, not just numbers into noise.

In the next chapter, we'll zoom in on **deal strategy and competitive execution**, because behind every forecast there is a portfolio of deals that must be orchestrated and won with precision.

Chapter 12: Winning Big Deals

"Big deals aren't won with heroics. They're won with orchestration."

Every GTM leader wants more big deals: high-ACV, multi-stakeholder, strategic wins that move the needle. But most teams treat big deals like bigger versions of small ones. They throw more time, more demos, and more discounts at them, hoping for a different result.

That's not strategy. That's gambling.

Winning large, complex deals requires a different level of rigor. It's not about doing more but about doing it **smarter, with precision and intent**. This chapter unpacks what the best teams do differently when the stakes are high.

The Stakes Are Different

Big deals impact not only numbers but the very trajectory of the organization. A single large win can change how the market perceives you, build internal confidence, and create momentum across teams. Specifically, they influence:

· Quarterly numbers and revenue predictability

· Rep and manager credibility with leadership

· Market visibility and reputation (especially when marquee logos are added)

· Future expansion potential, including cross-sell and upsell opportunities

But they also introduce complexity and risk:

· They **take much longer** than average deals, often spanning multiple quarters or years

· They **involve a web of stakeholders** across functions, geographies, and levels of authority

- They **attract heightened competition**, with rivals bringing their best resources to the table

- They **demand internal coordination** across Sales, Product, Legal, Finance, and Executive teams

- They **create higher stakes** for mistakes; missteps in alignment or communication can cost millions

This is why you don't simply "close" a big deal. You **engineer a win plan**, treating the pursuit as a structured program with milestones, owners, risk management, and executive sponsorship.

Multi-Threading: The Non-Negotiable

If your big deal has one contact, you don't have a deal, you just have a contact. Complex opportunities demand multiple access points and advocates inside the customer's organization. The risk of relying on a single person is immense: job changes, shifting priorities, or loss of influence can kill months of work overnight.

High-performing reps therefore:

- **Map the full buying committee** (economic buyers, technical evaluators, users, influencers, blockers, and hidden power brokers)

- **Build layered relationships** across departments and hierarchies, ensuring they understand motivations from executives down to end users

- **Create tailored value** for each stakeholder, not just the main champion, by connecting your solution to their specific goals and risks

- **Use mutual action plans** to drive aligned timelines and surface misalignment early

- **Leverage internal champions** to navigate political dynamics and broaden organizational support

Multi-threading isn't optional. It's a **risk mitigation strategy**, a win accelerator, and a way to make the deal resilient. The deeper and wider your reach inside the account, the harder it is for competitors to displace you and the stronger your probability of closing with confidence.

Deal Strategy: From Tactics to Architecture

Top reps build a **deal architecture** that provides structure and foresight, much like an architect's blueprint before breaking ground on a building. This architecture includes the following critical elements:

· **Pain and urgency**: Why now? What's driving action? Is it strong enough? How does this relate to the buyers involved? Top reps probe for not just surface-level pain but the organizational priorities and pressures (market shifts, executive mandates, regulatory deadlines) that can make or break urgency.

· **Value alignment**: How does this solve something meaningful for them? They translate features into financial impact, operational efficiency, or strategic differentiation, making sure the buyer sees measurable outcomes, not just a product.

· **Competitive positioning**: Why us vs. the others? This requires clarity on your differentiators and the courage to directly address competitor strengths. It's less about bashing competitors and more about reframing the buying criteria so your solution is advantaged.

· **Process clarity**: Do we understand their buying process and timeline? Top performers map stakeholders, approval gates, procurement cycles, and decision-making forums to anticipate obstacles rather than being surprised by them.

· **Internal alignment**: Have we marshaled the right internal support? Winning complex deals requires coordination with legal, Finance, product, executives, and customer success. Reps ensure internal champions are prepped and that their organization shows up with one voice.

Each of these elements needs **intentional coverage**, not just hope. Deal strategy becomes a living document; reviewed in deal reviews, adjusted as new information emerges, and used as a guide to orchestrate both customer-facing and internal actions. This is how top performers transform a collection of tactics into a cohesive win plan.

Competitive Execution

Big deals always attract competition. Competitors will bring their A-teams, often with aggressive pricing, bold claims, and heavy executive involvement. To prevail, you must elevate the conversation and compete in ways that transcend feature checklists and price wars. Beat them with:

· **Insights**: Teach your customers something new about their problem or opportunity. Share perspectives they haven't considered, such as industry benchmarks, emerging risks, or innovative approaches. Becoming a trusted advisor creates differentiation competitors can't easily replicate.

· **Differentiated proof points**: Bring hard evidence that validates your claims. This includes customer success stories that mirror the buyer's context, quantified business value tied to metrics that matter to them, and technical validations that remove doubt about feasibility and performance.

· **Executive engagement**: Orchestrate peer-to-peer conversations between your executives and theirs. This builds credibility at the highest levels, shows long-term commitment, and reduces perceived risk. Executive presence often tips the scale in complex, high-ACV decisions.

· **Counter-positioning**: Anticipate competitor strengths and reframe them in a way that highlights your unique advantage. Do this proactively and respectfully (without going negative) so you shape the buying criteria in your favor before rivals define the narrative.

· **Customer co-creation**: Involve the buyer in shaping the solution or implementation roadmap. When they co-own the design, they are less likely to be swayed by competitors later in the process.

Compete on **insight and value creation**, not features. The goal is to make the decision less about comparing vendors and more about choosing a partner who understands their business and can guide them to future success.

Team Selling and Internal Orchestration

Winning big deals requires cross-functional alignment across multiple disciplines. A single rep, no matter how talented, cannot bring the technical depth, financial creativity, executive credibility, and post-sale assurance that customers expect when making a multimillion-dollar decision. Follow examples of what different stakeholders bring to the table:

- **Solutions Engineering**: Deliver tailored demos, technical deep-dives, and proof-of-concepts that validate feasibility. They act as translators of complex technology into customer-specific solutions.

- **Customer Success**: Provide a clear post-sale plan, demonstrating how the customer will be supported from onboarding through expansion. Their involvement signals commitment to long-term value, not just the initial transaction.

- **Executive Sponsors**: Offer risk mitigation and relationship depth. When your C-suite engages with theirs, it elevates the partnership and reduces perceived risk for senior buyers.

- **Pricing/Finance**: Bring flexibility and creativity in structuring commercial terms without eroding value. They help balance customer demands with business economics.

- **Legal/Compliance**: For many enterprise deals, legal alignment can make or break timelines. Having engaged legal resources who understand both customer needs and your internal guardrails accelerates closure.

- **Product/Innovation Teams**: In strategic accounts, product input can help align roadmaps with customer priorities and signal commitment to joint innovation.

Use a **deal team model** to harness these functions:

- **Assign clear roles and responsibilities** throughout your sales process so every team member knows when and how to contribute

- **Create shared objectives** that tie the win to broader company goals (ARR growth, market penetration, reference accounts)

- **Run internal deal reviews**, strategy sessions, and dry-runs before key customer meetings to ensure alignment and readiness
- **Capture learnings** from each major pursuit and recycle them into playbooks for future deals

The rep is the quarterback, not the hero. Their role is to orchestrate the team, call the plays, and ensure flawless execution.

Mutual Action Plans: Shared Accountability

MAPs are underrated and underused, yet they can serve as the backbone of disciplined execution in complex deals. Done right, they:

- **Align buyer and seller timelines**, creating visibility into both sides' processes
- **Create shared milestones** that keep the deal moving forward in an accountable way
- **Surface delays or gaps** early so corrective actions can be taken before momentum is lost
- **Create deal momentum** by demonstrating progress and shared ownership

They also clarify roles and responsibilities on both sides, ensuring legal, procurement, technical, and executive stakeholders all know their part in the process. A well-run MAP becomes a joint project plan: one that fosters transparency, reduces surprises, and builds trust.

They're especially useful for deals with long procurement or legal cycles, regulatory oversight, or global coordination. Make it a standard for any deal over a certain threshold, and review it regularly in deal reviews to reinforce discipline and signal to the customer that you take execution as seriously as the sale itself.

Deal Reviews: Discipline in Action

Deal reviews are where strategy meets accountability. They are not forecast calls in disguise, but working sessions that pressure test the deal strategy, identify risks, and align resources. A strong deal review culture separates top-performing Sales organizations from those constantly surprised by lost opportunities.

Why they matter

· Provide visibility into deal health and gaps that need attention

· Ensure the rep is not operating in isolation but is benefiting from team expertise

· Align internal stakeholders on next steps, responsibilities, and risks

· Reinforce methodology and sales process discipline

· Create a safe but accountable environment where assumptions are challenged

· Provide developmental coaching moments for reps and managers alike

How to structure them

· **Preparation:** The rep submits a deal brief in advance (stage, stakeholders, pain, value, risks, competitive landscape, MAP status). This ensures the session is about problem-solving, not data-gathering.

· **Review format:**

 – Clarify deal objective and current stage

 – Inspect stakeholder map and level of multi-threading

 – Validate value proposition alignment with customer priorities

 – Assess competitive threats and counter-positioning

 – Review mutual action plan and timeline risks

 – Define next actions and owners

 – Capture risks and mitigation plans explicitly

· **Participants:** Rep, manager, solutions engineer, and any relevant cross-functional partners. For strategic accounts, include executive sponsors to add weight and perspective.

· **Cadence:** Weekly for top opportunities, monthly for broader pipeline coverage. Critical deals may warrant ad-hoc reviews when milestones or risks surface.

Deal reviews should feel like coaching and strategy sessions, not interrogations. The goal is to improve win probability, surface blind spots, and reduce surprises, not to simply check a box. Done consistently, they build a culture of rigor, transparency, and continuous improvement.

Wrap-Up: Big Deals Require Big Discipline

Big deals don't get won by accident. They require intentional design and disciplined orchestration across every dimension: multi-threading, deal strategy, competitive execution, team selling, mutual action plans, and rigorous deal reviews. They are as much about aligning your internal resources as they are about influencing the customer's decision-making process. Think of them as enterprise projects with executive sponsorship, risk management, and clear milestones, not as oversized transactions.

The organizations that consistently win these deals treat them with the same seriousness as launching a product or entering a new market. They build playbooks, run structured reviews, and invest in preparation and orchestration. In short, they apply project discipline to selling.

In the next chapter, we'll shift focus to the **Sales Manager**: the execution multiplier who ensures that process, pipeline, forecast, and deal discipline don't just exist at the top, but cascade effectively across every rep and every opportunity.

Chapter 13: The Modern Sales Rep - Where Strategy Meets the Customer

"No GTM plan survives first contact with the customer, unless it's executed by a well-prepared rep."

The Human Engine of GTM Execution

Every GTM plan ultimately depends on a single conversation: the one between a seller and a customer. That's the moment of truth where strategy meets reality.

The sales representative sits at the center of this moment. They are not just executors of process; they are interpreters of strategy, translating what the company *intends to do* into what the customer *is willing to buy.*

While technology, data, and AI have reshaped the sales landscape, the core mission of a great rep has not changed. It can be summed up in three verbs: **Create. Advance. Close.**

These are the building blocks of execution; the rhythm that turns strategy into revenue.

The Seller's Mission: Create, Advance, Close

Every sales methodology -from Challenger to MEDDICC- is simply a structured way to do three things better: **Create opportunities, advance them, and close them.**

- **Create**: Identify, qualify, and engage prospects that match your Ideal Customer Profile. The goal is to *earn the right to a conversation* and reveal needs worth solving.

- **Advance**: Move opportunities forward by guiding the customer's decision process, clarifying impact, and building internal consensus.

- **Close**: Convert intent into commitment and ensure a smooth transition to delivery and success.

Top performers execute these fundamentals consistently and with purpose. They understand that their success is not measured by how busy they look, but by how effectively they create momentum across these three stages. Anything else, is not a priority and should be ignored.

Manager's Corner: The Simplicity Test

If you ask your reps what their job is, and the answer doesn't include *create, advance, and close,* you've lost alignment. Keep the mission visible. Coach to it. Measure to it.

Creating Opportunities: Lead With a Powerful Message

Before any customer engagement begins, a rep must first **earn attention**, and that starts with the message.

In a world flooded with noise, prospects don't respond to product pitches; they respond to relevance. The most effective sellers lead with a message that connects directly to the **differentiated value proposition** defined earlier in the GTM plan and shaped by the Ideal Customer Profile (ICP). They understand exactly who they're talking to -the persona, their goals, and pain points- and tailor the outreach accordingly, ideally, guided by clear sales plays built around that persona.

Each outreach and call preparation session should connect strategy with execution: knowing the ICP, anticipating their challenges, and bringing insights that prove credibility.

This is where strategy meets reality: reps translating market insight and enablement frameworks into targeted, meaningful conversations that create value from the first touch.

That value proposition is not marketing copy; it's the rep's **conversation starter.** It tells the story of how you understand the world of a specific type of customer, why your solution matters to them, in language that speaks to their outcomes, not your features.

A powerful message answers three unspoken buyer questions immediately:

1. Do you understand my business?

2. Can you help me solve something that truly matters?

3. Why should I give you 30 minutes of my time?

Top reps internalize these points. They tailor outreach to show they know the customer's world by referencing industry challenges, trigger events, or recent moves that make the conversation timely. They connect the company's **value proposition** to the prospect's **business context**, closing the gap between strategy and execution in a single, clear statement.

Example: Instead of: "We help companies automate payroll processes." Say: "We help HR leaders eliminate compliance risk and reduce manual workload by 40%, freeing time for strategic initiatives that have bigger business impact."

This kind of messaging turns a cold email into a relevant insight. It reframes outreach from interruption to opportunity.

From Message to Conversation

Once the message earns engagement, the next step is to convert that initial spark into **dialogue**, and that's where **discovery** begins.

Discovery is not about checking qualification boxes. It's about validating and expanding the value hypothesis introduced in your message. The best reps approach it like an experiment:

We believe this customer faces X problem that causes Y impact. Let's explore if that's true and what it means for them.

This creates a natural transition from prospecting to exploration; from *talking at* the customer to *thinking with* them.

Manager's Corner: Message Discipline

Don't let messaging drift between Marketing and Sales. Every rep should be able to articulate the company's value proposition in one sentence, tailored to the buyer they're calling. Coach reps to *start with outcomes*, not features; and connect every outreach to a clear hypothesis of value.

Advancing Opportunities: The Power of the Middle

The middle of the funnel is where deals either gain momentum or stall. It's where curiosity must turn into confidence, both for the rep and the buyer.

Two capabilities separate elite performers:

Facilitating Consensus

Buying decisions are now made by groups, not individuals. Reps must help their champions navigate internal politics and align stakeholders.

This often requires mapping the entire decision ecosystem, understanding who influences, who approves, and who blocks progress. They act as internal project managers of the customer's decision process, orchestrating communication among diverse personas with different priorities.

Great sellers recognize that each stakeholder views value differently, so they tailor messages to connect with economic, technical, and operational buyers alike.

They also coordinate internal resources -such as solution engineers, pricing specialists, and Customer Success partners- to support the customer's buying process, ensuring expertise is available at every stage of evaluation.

They use account plans, stakeholder alignment maps, and mutual action plans to keep both internal and external teams synchronized, making it easier for the customer to buy and for the organization to deliver on its promises.

Presenting with Power

Presentations, demos, and proposals are where understanding becomes conviction. Powerful presentations follow a clear storyline:

1. The problem

2. The impact

3. The solution

4. The proof

5. The path forward

Presenting with power is not about theatrics. It's about **clarity, confidence, and conviction**, helping buyers visualize the outcome and feel confident advancing.

Manager's Corner: Coach for the Middle

Pipeline reviews often focus on what's new or what's about to close. Don't ignore the middle. That's where deals die or mature. Coach your team to identify stuck opportunities and define the *next advanceable action.*

Closing Opportunities: From Commitment to Confidence

Closing is not a high-pressure moment; it's the natural conclusion of alignment. When the process has been managed well, closing becomes about validation, not persuasion.

Strong closers:

· Remove friction before it becomes an obstacle.

· Engage Legal, Finance, and Success teams early.

· Confirm mutual understanding of value and next steps.

· Set expectations for implementation.

Closing isn't about pushing harder but about making it easier for the buyer to say yes with confidence.

Managing the Calendar and the Pipeline

Behind every consistent performer is **a disciplined calendar and a clean pipeline.**

A rep's **calendar** reveals their priorities. Top performers:

· Block time for prospecting every week.

· Prepare for customer meetings, not improvise them.

· Schedule follow-ups immediately, not "when they have time."

· Balance time between active deals and pipeline generation.

A rep's **pipeline** reveals their business. It's both a mirror (showing what is real) and a map (showing where to go next). Healthy pipelines are:

· Accurate in stage definitions

· Regularly updated

· Aligned to clear coverage and velocity goals

When the calendar and pipeline are well managed, predictability follows. Discipline becomes freedom.

Manager's Corner: Make the Calendar a Coaching Tool

Don't just review the pipeline. When performance lacks, review the week. Ask:

· "Where do you create?"

· "What are you advancing?"

· "Which deals are ready to close?"

This rhythm keeps coaching grounded in execution, not activity.

The Rep as the Catalyst of GTM Execution

Every enablement program, process redesign, and RevOps investment exists to make the rep better at these fundamentals. They are the living embodiment of the GTM system. When they execute with clarity and discipline, growth follows. When they struggle, it reveals where planning, alignment, or enablement need reinforcement.

The modern rep is more than a messenger of value; they are a *creator of value*, shaping how customers perceive outcomes and how companies realize them.

Key Takeaways

Principle	Description
Create, Advance, Close	The timeless rhythm of sales success. Every activity should serve one of these three outcomes.
Lead With Message, Not Product	A differentiated value proposition is the rep's most powerful engagement tool.
Great Discovery = Great Deals	Discovery is not about qualification; it's about insight and trust.
Present With Power	Communicate impact with clarity, confidence, and conviction.
Calendar + Pipeline = Control	Time discipline and pipeline hygiene are the twin engines of predictability.
The Rep Is the GTM Catalyst	Every strategy lives or dies through the quality of its execution at the point of customer contact.

Wrap-Up

The fundamentals of selling have not changed; they've simply become more demanding. Reps today must master the blend of process, empathy, and data that turns potential into performance.

At its core, selling remains the art of turning strategy into action, one customer conversation at a time. That's the essence of GTM execution.

As the next chapter will show, this execution doesn't happen in isolation. The sales manager plays a pivotal role as the multiplier of performance, transforming individual effort into team consistency. Where reps bring strategy to life in customer conversations, managers amplify it through focus, coaching, and accountability. Together, they turn the GTM system into measurable, scalable growth.

Chapter 14: Sales Manager as Execution Multiplier

"If you want to scale excellence, coach the coaches."

When execution breaks down in the field, most organizations look at reps. But the real leverage point -the one that scales performance, consistency, and culture- is the frontline sales manager.

Sales managers are the most critical (and most overlooked!) leverage point in your GTM model.

They are not just team leads. They are force multipliers. Execution engines. They are the *scalers* of rep effectiveness.

But here's the issue: we expect them to manage forecasts, coach reps, onboard new hires, run team meetings, enforce process, deliver numbers, and retain talent, all with little to no enablement of their own.

It's backward. And it's costing organizations millions in productivity and missed revenue.

This chapter is about turning sales managers into **force multipliers**, not just administrators.

Redefining the Role: From Firefighter to Coach

Sales managers sit at the execution layer where strategy meets reality. They're responsible for driving consistency across teams, accelerating performance, and embedding discipline into daily sales motion.

They influence:

- How fast reps ramp skills
- How well reps qualify opportunities
- How deals are coached
- Which reps grow (or churn)
- Whether the sales motion actually lands in the field

They touch **every deal, every rep, every day.**

And yet most companies promote managers based on individual performance and then hand them the key... Without a playbook.

Too many managers are stuck in a reactive loop:

· Approving discounts

· Running reports

· Chasing CRM updates

· Jumping on late-stage calls

This is **sales support**, not **sales management**.

High-impact managers do three things consistently:

1. **Inspect pipeline, process, and performance**

2. **Develop rep skills through structured coaching**

3. **Hold reps accountable for their performance**

Everything else is secondary, or should be delegated.

The Manager Operating Rhythm

Managers' operating rhythm serves as a space where they execute their core activities: inspect, coach, and hold reps accountable.

Structure enables focus. Build a manager cadence anchored in execution. Here's an example:

Cadence	Focus	Format
Weekly	1:1s, pipeline inspection, deal coaching, call plan reviews, and joint customer calls	Rep-specific sessions
Biweekly	Team meeting: wins, blockers, skill focus	Group session
Monthly	Forecast accountability, metrics review	Review with leadership
Quarterly	Rep performance reviews, hiring calibration	Manager enablement session

Managers shouldn't invent their rhythm. It should be designed and institutionalized by Sales leadership.

Turning Rhythm into Coaching Moments

A manager's operating rhythm creates the structure and consistency needed for performance. But rhythm alone doesn't create growth. The real impact comes from how managers use those touchpoints. Every 1:1, pipeline inspection, or team meeting is a chance to connect with what reps are doing and help them do it even better. These moments of interaction are where coaching lives and where culture is shaped.

Coming out of discussions on cadence and rhythm, it becomes clear that the heartbeat of a manager's impact lies not in scheduling the meeting, but in how they engage during it. A well-structured operating rhythm creates the space for managers to plug into rep activity, and each of those interactions is an opportunity to sharpen skills, reinforce process, and elevate performance.

Too often, when those opportunities arise, managers fall back on the most basic form of feedback: telling. "You should have done X." While well-intentioned, this type of directive response is limiting. It shuts down reflection and reduces the chance for reps to think through their actions, ultimately stunting their ability to grow beyond simply following orders. This is not coaching...

Real coaching sounds different:

- "What did you notice in that meeting?"

- "What was the customer really trying to solve?"

- "What could we do differently next time?"

These questions invite reps to think critically about their actions and the customer's perspective. They also give managers insight into how reps process information and where blind spots may exist.

Coaching means:

- **Diagnosing skill gaps** based on observable behaviors, not just outcomes

- **Role-playing key moments** in the sales cycle to prepare for real-world scenarios

- **Reinforcing methodology-aligned behaviors** so reps develop consistent habits

- **Holding reps accountable for improvement**, with clear expectations and follow-ups

- **Encouraging reps to self-assess** and articulate their own learning, which deepens ownership of results

Most successful organizations at embedding a sales coaching culture use standardized frameworks and equip managers with toolkits that include coaching guides, conversation prompts, and scoring rubrics. They also build coaching into the operating rhythm, treating it as a core responsibility, not an optional activity squeezed in when time allows.

They coach the **thinking**, not just the action. This distinction matters: when reps learn how to think through situations, they become more adaptable, resilient, and capable of handling complex deals. The coaching environment should be safe for reflection, yet firmly accountable to outcomes, striking a balance between support and performance pressure.

1:1s That Drive Performance

Not all 1:1s are the same. In fact, the highest-performing managers deliberately separate two distinct types of meetings:

- **Accountability 1:1s**

- **Personal Development 1:1s**

Blending the two dilutes their impact; clarity of purpose is what makes each one powerful.

Accountability 1:1s (Results, Pipeline, Activity)

The accountability 1:1 is the manager's meeting (not the rep's). Its sole purpose is accountability. It should be short, fact-based, and focused on the progression of results, pipeline, and activity (in this specific order).

- Managers review results against goals and relative performance compared to peers.

- They inspect overall pipeline health.

- They ask two powerful questions each week:

  - What **new opportunities** have you **created** since our last accountability meeting?

  - Which **existing opportunities** have you **advanced**?

- If the results and pipeline are insufficient, managers proceed to inspect the activity. They do not allow the rep to deflect or turn the tables. This is not a coaching session.

- They keep the discussion data-driven, not emotional. The facts speak for themselves; no need for raised voices or conflict.

- They never skip this meeting, even with top performers. At 15 minutes a week, it is the single highest-payoff Sales management activity. Something else should be canceled before canceling this.

When conducted consistently, this meeting reinforces discipline. It creates a culture where performance is visible, progress is expected, and excuses do not replace execution.

Personal Development 1:1s (Growth, Skills, Career)

Separate from accountability, these 1:1s are the manager's best opportunity to move beyond inspection into meaningful development. They are private, consistent, and rep-focused, making them the perfect forum for skill growth and personal alignment. These conversations should take place at least once a month.

Great personal development 1:1s focus on:

- **Skill gaps and development plans**: identifying competencies to strengthen, outlining practice strategies, and tracking improvement.

- **Deal and call coaching**: role-playing scenarios, diagnosing behaviors, and reinforcing methodology.

- **Personal goals and well-being**: building trust by showing interest in the rep as a whole person, not just a producer of numbers.

· **Long-term career growth**: helping reps see pathways and preparing them for expanded responsibilities.

Strong managers use these coaching sessions to earn the right to be seen not just as scorekeepers but as true developers of talent. They avoid turning them into forecast updates or accountability reviews. The development 1:1 is about **growth, not reporting**. It is where reps sharpen their thinking, expand their skills, and build confidence for the next level.

Call Planning

Call planning is one of the most overlooked disciplines in sales, yet it has a disproportionate impact on performance. Every customer interaction - whether a discovery call, demo, or executive meeting- deserves preparation. Preparation signals respect, builds confidence, and allows reps to shape the conversation rather than simply react to it.

A good call plan addresses the following:

· **WHY are you having this meeting?** The answer to this question should be around the high-level purpose of the meeting and connected to the exit criteria of the stage of your sales process the opportunity is in.

· **What do you want to ACHIEVE?** This should provide the tangible outcomes to be achieved during the meeting and serve as the reference to evaluate success.

· **HOW do you plan to achieve this?** This is where you should get how clear is the rep on the agenda and how to drive it.

· **What is the CONTEXT of this meeting?** This can be a follow-up question to understand, among other things, how we got to this meeting, who is attending, and what can be in their minds coming to the meeting.

· **What can PREVENT you from achieving the planned results?** This one can be a very powerful question to assess whether different scenarios have been considered by the salesperson (and trigger some thoughts if this wasn't the case).

Sales managers play a critical role here. They should inspect rep call plans in 1:1s and deal reviews, insist that a call plan exists for every customer meeting they attend, coach on the quality of preparation, and model the behavior by preparing their own call plans for customer interactions. Over time, this raises the standard across the team and creates a culture where preparation is expected and valued, not optional.

Hiring and Talent Development

Hiring and talent development are among the most critical responsibilities of a sales manager, yet they are seldom taught, especially to managers who were promoted directly from a rep role. Most new managers inherit hiring responsibilities without guidance on how to assess potential, build balanced teams, or accelerate ramp. The result is that talent decisions often default to intuition instead of structured evaluation.

The best managers, by contrast, become **talent spotters and builders**. They:

- **Know what "great" looks like** for their segment and can articulate the traits that predict success

- **Participate actively in recruiting and onboarding**, ensuring cultural and skill fit from the very start

- **Own ramp plans and success metrics**, treating early performance as a joint accountability between rep and manager

- **Identify who's ready to stretch and who needs intervention**, applying coaching or corrective action as needed

- **Build succession pipelines**, preparing future leaders and top performers rather than just filling today's gaps

Your future top performers are either being built (or lost!) by your managers today. Equipping managers with the skills to hire, ramp, and develop people effectively is one of the highest-leverage investments an organization can make.

Enable the Manager to Enable Others

Sales Enablement often focuses on reps. But managers need enablement, too. In fact, this is one of the most overlooked areas of investment, even though managers are the multipliers of performance across teams. Equipping them with the right tools, frameworks, and peer support is critical if you want consistent execution across the field.

Sales manager enablement should cover:

· **Training on coaching models** so that feedback moves from telling to developing

· **Access to insights** that show patterns across team performance, helping managers diagnose issues at scale

· **Content and plays** they can reinforce in the field, ensuring alignment between enablement and execution

· **Hiring and developing talent**, giving them structured guidance on assessing, onboarding, and ramping new reps

· **Driving and managing change**, since managers are the first line of leadership when new processes or tools are rolled out

· **Peer forums** to share what's working, creating a community of practice across managers

If you want consistency across teams, start by standardizing how your managers lead. This is not a one-time training but an ongoing enablement journey. We will go deeper into what a comprehensive sales manager enablement program looks like in the **Revenue Enablement** chapters of this book, where the focus shifts to how organizations build the infrastructure that equips both reps and managers for sustainable success.

Wrap-Up: Scale Through the Middle

You can't scale a Sales org by coaching every rep yourself. The math simply doesn't work. But you can scale a high-performance culture by investing in your managers, the true multipliers of execution. They touch every deal, every rep, and every process daily. When equipped with the right rhythm, coaching skills, hiring discipline, and enablement support, managers become the engine that drives consistency, accountability, and growth at scale.

The lesson from this chapter is clear: excellence doesn't cascade by chance. It cascades through managers who are trained, empowered, and held to the same standard of discipline that we expect from our frontline. Organizations that enable their managers not only unlock higher rep performance but also create the leadership bench strength needed for long-term success.

With GTM Execution complete, we now turn to Revenue Enablement, the third pillar of GTM Excellence. This is where we explore how to equip, activate, and scale the capabilities that sustain execution across both reps and managers.

Part III: Revenue Enablement

Chapter 15: Strategic Enablement

"Enablement isn't support. It's how strategy shows up in the field."

Most organizations still treat Enablement as a service function: onboarding, training logistics, maybe a few sales decks. That mindset leaves Enablement stuck in reactive mode, executing requests instead of driving outcomes.

But the role of Enablement has evolved. In high-performing GTM organizations, Enablement is a **strategic engine** that connects corporate goals with field execution. It's not about delivering content. It's about equipping people to perform. At scale. With consistency. And impact.

This chapter defines what strategic enablement is, and what it looks like in practice

Enablement as a Strategic GTM Capability

The last few years, especially in B2B SaaS and enterprise sales, have forced a transformation.

Buyers are more sophisticated. Deals are more complex. Sales motions require tight orchestration across functions. And CROs can't afford to run fragmented, inefficient GTM teams.

Strategic enablement stepped in to solve for that complexity. Not by doing more training, but by rethinking **how organizations equip their teams to execute**.

Modern enablement is:

· Proactive, not reactive

· Embedded in revenue strategy, not adjacent to it

· Accountable to outcomes, not just activity

· Operationally rigorous and data-informed

What Strategic Enablement Actually Looks Like

Let's make this concrete. Strategic enablement doesn't just "support" revenue teams, it helps them *win*. Here's how.

1. Deep Integration with GTM Strategy

Enablement starts where GTM strategy starts: target segments, ideal customer profiles, key problems we solve, and how we differentiate.

It works in partnership with Sales, CS, Marketing, and RevOps to:

· Translate strategy into field execution

· Operationalize messaging and plays

· Drive cross-functional alignment across the funnel

This isn't about pushing content. It's about making strategy executable.

2. Owns and Influences Core Productivity Metrics

Strategic enablement teams are measured by **outcomes**, not participation. Metrics like:

· Time to ramp

· Time to first deal

· Quota attainment

· Pipeline conversion at each stage

They don't just report on these, they build programs and interventions to move them.

3. Partners with RevOps to Build a Data-Driven Enablement Engine

RevOps and Enablement are natural allies. Together, they build systems of insight and execution.

RevOps brings visibility. Enablement turns insights into actions:

· "Why are we losing late-stage deals?" → Enablement develops objection-handling training and deal reviews.

· "Stage 2 conversion is dropping?" → Enablement refines discovery talk tracks and prospecting frameworks.

When these two functions are aligned, GTM teams are faster, smarter, and more adaptable.

4. Drives Coaching as a Force Multiplier

Manager enablement is often the missing piece. Strategic enablement empowers front-line managers to coach to behaviors that actually drive deals forward, not just forecast calls and activity reviews.

This creates consistency across the field and ensures that every rep isn't reinventing the wheel on their way to quota.

5. Designs Enablement Programs that Scale

As orgs grow, complexity increases. Strategic enablement builds repeatable systems for onboarding, product launches, methodology adoption, and change management, without slowing down execution.

The goal: consistency without rigidity.

Why This Matters Now

Most companies are under pressure to **do more with less**. Growth expectations haven't dropped, but headcount, budgets, and buyer urgency have.

This puts a spotlight on **execution quality**. Not just "do we have enough reps?" but "are our reps equipped to win against better-prepared competitors?"

That's Enablement's moment.

Companies that embed enablement into their GTM DNA will:

· Ramp reps faster

· Win more deals at higher ASPs

· Retain more customers

· Execute consistently across regions and segments

· Launch new offerings without a 6-month lag in field readiness

Companies that don't? They'll burn cycles, miss targets, and struggle to scale.

Pillars of a Strategic Enablement Model

A scalable, effective Enablement function is built on five pillars:

1. Onboarding & Ramp Acceleration

Role-specific onboarding is the first true test of Enablement's ability to deliver impact. Compressing time-to-productivity means going beyond orientation slides. It requires structured 30-60-90-day plans, integrated field practice, manager accountability, and outcome-based certifications. Effective ramping programs ensure that new hires contribute to pipeline faster, reducing both opportunity cost and attrition risk.

2. Skills Development & Coaching

Knowledge without reinforcement fades quickly. The goal of Enablement is to drive consistent, repeatable seller behaviors. This is achieved by mapping skills to roles, delivering structured practice, and validating with formal certification. Skills development is not just training events; it's a cycle of exposure, application, coaching, and feedback that produces measurable improvements in win rates and deal velocity.

3. Sales Plays & Field Activation

Sales plays translate strategy into action in the field. A strong Enablement function arms reps with just-in-time tools -talk tracks, persona-based guides, objection handling, proof points- embedded into workflows. Activation means roleplays, deal reviews, and campaigns that make plays part of the operating cadence, ensuring strategy doesn't remain a slide deck but shows up in real customer conversations.

4. Manager Enablement

Frontline managers are the ultimate multipliers of enablement. Equipping managers with coaching frameworks, scorecards, and structured cadences ensures that skills and plays are reinforced in the field. Manager enablement isn't an optional extra; it embeds accountability into daily execution and helps managers become talent developers, not just deal chasers.

5. Measurement & Feedback Loops

What gets measured gets improved. Enablement must tie efforts to leading indicators such as time-to-first deal, stage conversion rates, play adoption, and coaching quality. Feedback loops with reps and managers help refine programs, ensuring they stay relevant and outcome-focused. Measurement makes Enablement a business driver, not a cost center.

Each pillar reinforces execution. Together, they form the foundation for scalable growth.

Organizational Design and Governance

Where Enablement sits matters. High-impact Enablement teams are designed intentionally, with structure and alignment that reflects their strategic importance to the business. The org design signals to the field whether Enablement is a tactical support function or a core driver of revenue performance.

Modern Enablement functions:

- **Report directly to a revenue leader** (CRO or Head of Sales), or at minimum have a dotted-line into both Sales and RevOps, ensuring accountability to revenue outcomes.

- **Are resourced by segment** (Enterprise, Mid-Market, Channel) so that enablement content and programs map to the realities of different deal sizes, buyer groups, and motions.

- **Have dedicated program owners for major initiatives** like onboarding, sales plays, and manager enablement. These owners bring focus, treat programs like products, and ensure continuous improvement.

· **Partner closely with Marketing, Product, and Operations** to align messaging, product launches, and sales process execution, creating a unified go-to-market rhythm.

In addition, strong Enablement teams often establish advisory councils with sales managers and frontline reps to gather input, test programs, and keep initiatives grounded in field reality.

Avoid Enablement being buried in HR or Learning & Development orgs. Those functions focus on general career development. Enablement is different: it requires deep commercial expertise and constant connection to revenue priorities. You're not building generalists, you're building experts who directly shape field performance.

From Content Factory to Performance Partner

Enablement isn't about delivering more decks. It's about improving sales performance and shaping field behavior. That requires moving beyond creating content to being embedded in the operating fabric of the business. Strategic Enablement teams become true partners by:

· **Partnering in QBRs** to identify capability gaps, not only reporting what happened but recommending programs to fix them.

· **Working with RevOps** to correlate enablement with pipeline health, stage conversions, and win rates, ensuring training and plays are tied to measurable outcomes.

· **Collaborating with Marketing** so that messaging and assets resonate with buyers, creating alignment between campaigns and field execution, and ensuring feedback from the field loops back into content creation.

· **Aligning with Product** to train the field on what matters most to customers and partners, prioritizing business impact rather than a flood of feature updates.

· **Engaging with Customer Success** leaders to ensure enablement extends beyond the first sale, driving adoption, retention, and expansion conversations.

This is the shift from a content factory to a **performance partner**, one that is accountable for changing behaviors and accelerating results. Strategic Enablement is a field-facing, insight-driven business function that translates strategy into execution and drives measurable impact.

AI Changes the Game - And Raises the Bar for Enablement

Here's the reality: **knowledge is no longer a differentiator**.

GenAI tools can generate content, summarize insights, prep call plans, and even draft personalized outreach, all in seconds. What used to be a competitive edge (access to information, playbooks, and templates) is now table stakes.

So, where does Enablement fit?

Right at the intersection of **strategy and execution**.

Reps don't need more knowledge; they need **better context, sharper judgment, and true business acumen**. They need to understand the customer's strategic objectives, not just product features. They need to navigate consensus buyers and build business cases that tie directly to outcomes.

That's what AI *can't* do on its own.

Enablement's new role is to:

· Teach reps how to **think**, not just what to say

· Equip managers to coach for **decision quality**, not activity volume

· Embed **customer-centric, outcome-focused thinking** across the GTM org

AI accelerates execution, but only if the underlying judgment, messaging, and strategy alignment are already strong. Otherwise, it just automates bad habits.

Enablement is now the function responsible for building that strategic muscle at scale.

This can include:

- Micro-coaching and just-in-time knowledge embedded in workflows
- AI-curated roleplays and feedback
- Personalized learning paths based on performance data
- Content surfacing based on deal context

The future of Enablement isn't just smarter content. It's **performance intelligence** delivered at the point of action.

Wrap-Up: From Reactive to Revenue Driver

Enablement is no longer optional, and it's not a cost center. It has become a strategic imperative for GTM teams that need to execute at scale with clarity, accountability, and adaptability. When built intentionally, Enablement becomes the connective tissue linking **strategy, field behavior, customer outcomes, and results**.

This means it is measured not by activity but by its impact on ramp speed, deal execution, manager effectiveness, and overall revenue performance. With AI raising the bar on what information is available, Enablement must now provide the context, judgment, and coaching infrastructure that technology cannot replace.

In the next chapter, we'll go deeper into **Onboarding and Ramp Acceleration**, because growth depends not only on hiring talent, but on how quickly they are equipped, coached, and ready to produce.

Chapter 16: Onboarding and Ramp Acceleration

"You don't have a hiring problem. You have a ramp problem."

Onboarding and ramp acceleration is the first of the enablement pillars introduced in *Chapter 15: Strategic Enablement*, and for good reason: it sets the foundation for all the others. Without a disciplined approach to onboarding, skills development, sales plays, and manager enablement will all struggle to take hold. Ramp speed is the first and most visible proof point of Enablement's impact on revenue.

Hiring great reps is only half the battle. Getting them productive, quickly, is where growth either compounds or stalls. Yet many companies still treat onboarding like an orientation exercise: a week of presentations, a product walkthrough, and a checklist. Then they throw the rep into the field and hope for the best.

That's not onboarding. That's negligence, and it comes at a huge opportunity cost.

Real onboarding is not a classroom event. It's a **performance acceleration system** that reduces time-to-revenue, builds confidence, and drives consistency across the team. It is how you turn talent into impact faster, by blending structured learning, live practice, manager certification and coaching, and in-flow reinforcement.

Strong onboarding programs connect directly to GTM strategy. They define the critical outcomes new hires must achieve, the milestones that prove readiness, and the metrics that track progress. They don't just answer *"what do reps need to know?"* but *"what do reps need to be able to do in their first 30, 60, and 90 days?"*

This chapter breaks down how to design and operationalize onboarding as a growth engine, not a compliance exercise.

The Cost of Slow Ramp

Every month a rep isn't producing, the costs ripple across the business:

- You're **burning quota coverage** and missing planned bookings.
- You're **losing pipeline momentum** as opportunities stall without ownership.
- You're **eroding confidence:** from the rep, their manager, and your CFO, who sees productivity assumptions slipping.
- You're **straining other team members** who must pick up the slack, creating uneven performance.

And it adds up fast. For a rep with a $1M quota and 6-month ramp, every 30-day delay costs roughly $83K in lost bookings; and that figure compounds when multiple hires are behind schedule.

Onboarding is not a "nice to have." It's a **growth and margin lever**, directly tied to revenue predictability, investor confidence, and long-term scalability.

What Ramp Should Measure

Ramp isn't just time in seat. Define and track:

- **Time to first meeting**: How long it takes a new seller to book and hold their first qualified customer conversation, an early indicator of activity ramp.
- **Time to first opportunity created**: The elapsed time until a seller successfully generates and enters a qualified sales opportunity in the CRM, showing their ability to progress beyond introductory meetings.
- **Time to first deal closed:** The period until the rep closes their first sale, demonstrating practical application of training and signaling early revenue contribution.
- **Time to full productivity (quota attainment rate)**: The time required for a seller to consistently achieve expected performance

levels, typically measured by hitting their full quota or run-rate bookings.

Set role-specific ramp benchmarks based on:

- Segment (SMB vs. Enterprise)

- Motion (inbound vs. outbound)

- Experience level (tenured vs. new-to-industry)

Keep track of how the different onboarding cohorts perform against the above metrics. This will help you track the impact of the changes you make to your onboarding program.

Make this a core dashboard in your RevOps stack.

Designing Role-Specific Onboarding

One-size-fits-all doesn't work. Effective onboarding programs are designed with intention and connected directly to the GTM process:

- **Tailored by role** (AE, SDR, CSM, SE, Partner Manager) so that each onboarding path reflects the actual activities and outcomes expected from that role.

- **Modular**: Delivered in short sprints over 30-60-90 days, creating natural checkpoints and reinforcement moments.

- **Outcome-based**: Tied to measurable milestones such as first customer meeting, first opportunity created, or first deal closed, not just content completion.

The sales process mapped in *Chapter 8: Sales Process as Competitive Advantage* should serve as the blueprint for onboarding and ongoing development. Each stage of that process provides clarity on which roles must do what, the knowledge they need, and the tools they must master to succeed.

Each phase of onboarding should deliberately combine knowledge, skills, tools, and a certification criterion to validate readiness. For a sales rep, this could look like:

· **Knowledge**: Deep understanding of product capabilities, industry context, and competitive landscape.

· **Skills**: Core selling motions like discovery, objection handling, positioning, and navigating multi-stakeholder deals.

· **Tools**: Proficiency in CRM, sales engagement platforms, forecasting systems, and any digital sales rooms used to engage buyers.

· **Certification**: Practical demonstrations such as live call simulations, peer roleplays, and formal manager sign-off.

Narratively, this means treating onboarding like training a pilot, not a tourist. Pilots don't just watch slides, they log flight hours, practice in simulators, and pass rigorous checks before taking control. Reps deserve the same rigor: structured practice, validated competence, and the confidence that they are truly ready to perform in front of customers.

Manager Involvement is Non-Negotiable

Managers are the ones who translate enablement into field execution. Without managers reinforcing behaviors and signing off skill proficiency, onboarding quickly unravels. Enablement runs the program. But **managers own the outcome**.

High-performing orgs ensure:

· **Managers are trained** on how to support onboarding, with clear expectations for their role in accelerating ramp and certifying skills.

· **Weekly check-ins** are structured, tracked, and focused on progress against ramp milestones rather than generic status updates.

· **Managers reinforce what's taught** with live coaching, helping reps apply concepts in customer-facing situations and correcting behaviors early.

· **Ramp plans are reviewed** jointly between Enablement and Sales leadership to maintain alignment on goals, progress, and necessary adjustments.

· **Managers are equipped with frameworks** for running call planning sessions, conducting deal reviews, and holding reps accountable in consistent cadences.

If managers aren't engaged, reps will revert to bad habits fast, and the investment in onboarding quickly erodes.

Pro tip: The best onboarding programs ensure that the final deliverable truly "meets customer expectations". In this case, the "customers" are the frontline managers of the onboarded candidates. If they do not certify that new hires can execute the activities expected of them, onboarding risks losing credibility and impact. Making managers the certifiers embeds accountability and creates a closed loop between enablement design and field execution.

Just-in-Time Support Beats Just-in-Case Training

Don't overload new reps with everything on day one. Instead, think of onboarding as building blocks of confidence and competence. Each layer should prepare the rep for the next, creating momentum rather than overwhelm.

· Deliver **baseline enablement** pre-day 1 (tools access, intro modules) so that reps arrive ready to engage rather than wasting their first week on admin.

· Focus initial onboarding on **first actions** (calls, demos, emails) that create early wins and accelerate confidence. This sets the tone that productivity, not passive learning, is the goal.

· Provide **in-flow resources** (objection handling cards, persona guides, call snippets) so reps can access support at the exact moment of need, turning learning into action.

· Layer complexity over time with **contextual learning**, introducing more advanced skills and knowledge as reps build competence and face real-world scenarios.

· Incorporate **manager reinforcement** by having managers guide reps through these stages, inspecting usage of resources, coaching first calls, and holding them accountable for execution.

Make content accessible at the point of need, not buried in a LMS. Think in terms of micro-learning, searchable assets, and AI-driven surfacing of content in CRM workflows. The more natural and frictionless the support, the faster new hires will absorb and apply it.

Measuring and Iterating Your Ramp Engine

Track performance over cohorts, not just individuals. Looking at data by cohort allows you to see whether the overall system is improving, not just whether one strong rep got lucky. Monitor things like:

- **Are reps ramping faster over time?** If the answer is no, then the onboarding design isn't compounding value, but stagnant.

- **Which managers consistently outperform in ramp?** Manager involvement is one of the biggest levers; if some outperform while others lag, that signals a coaching or accountability gap.

- **Which onboarding components correlate with faster productivity?** For example, do roleplays shorten time to first deal? Does early customer exposure accelerate confidence?

- **Where are reps getting stuck?** Are they stalling before first meetings, or failing to progress opportunities beyond discovery?

Cohort performance, manager ramp variance, component impact, failure points; all of these should be visible in dashboards. **Treat onboarding like a** product: launch, measure, iterate. Use the data to identify what to scale, what to fix, and what to stop.

Onboarding isn't a project, it's a permanent GTM asset and one of the most important levers for revenue predictability.

Wrap-Up: Build Ramp Like a Product

You wouldn't make a new release, whether it's a new software or an industrial product, without instrumentation, quality checks, and a plan for continuous improvement.

Why would you do it with your onboarding process?

138

Treat it like a living system that is constantly monitored, measured, and refined, not a one-time training event.

Every day a new hire isn't selling is a day you're missing revenue. But the impact is larger than missed quota. It affects pipeline health, team morale, and investor confidence. Onboarding is the lever that turns talent into contribution, strategy into execution, and hiring into growth. Build it like it matters... Because it does.

Chapter 17: Skills Development and Coaching

"If you want consistent results, build consistent sellers."

Sales isn't just a talent game. It's a capability game. You don't scale revenue by hiring unicorns; you scale it by building a team that knows how to execute, every day, in every deal. Talent may get you early wins, but **capabilities are the true currency traded by Enablement**: they are what compounding growth is built on.

And that takes more than onboarding. It takes **systematic, ongoing skills development**. Not ad-hoc training. Not inspirational speakers. But structured programs tied directly to how the business sells, how buyers actually purchase, and what the customer expects in every interaction.

Enablement's role is to convert raw potential into durable capabilities that can be demonstrated, measured, and reinforced. The goal is not just to make reps smarter but to make them consistently better performers who can deliver in varied contexts.

This chapter is about making coaching and skills development a durable competitive advantage; not a quarterly initiative or a one-off project, but the foundation for repeatable, scalable revenue execution.

From Knowledge to Capability Building

Many teams confuse knowledge with skill, and most stop there. But enablement is about building **capabilities**: the higher-order combination of skills that allow a seller to perform consistently under varied conditions.

- **Knowledge** is knowing what to do.

- **Skill** is being able to do it under pressure.

- **Capability** is the architecture that bundles multiple skills into a repeatable strength a role can rely on to execute consistently.

A well-defined capability framework provides that architecture. It identifies the capabilities required by a role, breaks each capability into a series of underpinning skills, and defines levels of proficiency for those skills. Skill proficiency levels definitions could look like this:

Level	Description
1. Basic Awareness	Demonstrates only initial understanding of a skill; requires guidance to apply it.
2 . Developing	Shows experience and progress; can apply the skill in controlled situations.
3 . Proficient	Consistently applies the skill in live situations, integrating it into deal strategy and execution.
4. Expert /Teacher	Demonstrates mastery; leverages the skill to influence outcomes and can teach or coach others effectively.

For example, when this architecture is applied to define the **Business Acumen** capability required by sales reps. It can be described through three key skills:

· **Business functional knowledge**: understanding customer business models, functions, and how decisions are made.

· **Industry, market & competitor knowledge**: awareness of industry trends, competitor positioning, and how external pressures shape customer priorities.

· **Company's products and services knowledge**: clarity on how your solutions align with customer needs, and how they compare in the market.

Putting it all together, the **Business Acumen** capability for a sales rep could be defined like this:

Capability: Business Acumen

Definition: Knows how business works in both broad, generic terms and targeted, customer-specific terms with business functional knowledge; industry, market & competitor knowledge; and the Company's products & services knowledge.

142

Skill definitions and proficiency levels would be as follows:

Skill	Definition	Level 1	Level 2	Level 3	Level 4
Business functional knowledge	Knowledge of how the customer's business and its functions work in broad, generic terms and targeted, customer-specific terms.	Can describe, at a high level, how a business operates and generates value.	Understands key mission and challenges for relevant personas in target accounts.	Proactively identifies business challenges for relevant stakeholders within target accounts.	Coaches others on identifying a wide variety of business challenges by industry and role.
Industry, market & competitor knowledge	Ability to understand the wider industry ecosystem, including industry reports and trends.	Knows where to find information on current industry, market, and competitive landscape for accounts in the territory	Describes current industry, market trends, and key competitors for accounts in the territory	Researches and translates emerging trends in the market and industry into potential insights for target accounts	Acts as a local go-to resource for industry and market insights to grow new business.
Company's products & services knowledge	Knowledge of the Company's product & services suite (features & benefits) and how they compare within the industry.	Can describe, at a high level, the Company's product offerings and their key differentiating features and associated benefits.	Can articulate how the Company is competitively differentiated in every sector/industry in the territory.	Uses compelling business cases to position the Company's products and services as solutions to target stakeholders' business goals.	Successfully tailors the Company's business case and value proposition to win highly complex and/or unique deals.

By defining capabilities and their supporting skills in a structured way, and measuring them consistently, organizations can identify which ones have the **strongest correlation with business outcomes**. This insight makes it possible **to target and prioritize enablement initiatives** that close gaps and accelerate performance.

Defining the Core Skill Set by Role

Each role requires a distinct capability mix. By mapping capabilities to roles and assigning target proficiency levels (L1–L4), organizations create clarity on what "good" looks like and how to measure progress.

Think of the capability framework as a pantry of ingredients where Beach capability is an ingredient, and the target proficiency levels define the proportions in which they are mixed to create the perfect recipe for each role. A Sales Development Rep may need more of the 'prospecting spice' and a touch of 'qualification depth,' while a Customer Success Manager requires a heavier dose of 'adoption orchestration' and 'value realization.' The art of enablement lies in defining and blending these ingredients just right so that every role produces consistent, high-quality outcomes.

An example of capabilities and expected proficiency levels for different roles could look like this:

Role	Capabilities & Target Proficiency Levels
Account Executives (AEs)	Business Acumen (L3), Discovery & Qualification (L3), Value Articulation (L3), Multi-threading & Buying Group Navigation (L3), Negotiation & Closing (L2–L3)
Sales Development Reps (SDRs)	Prospecting Strategy (L3), Personalization & Relevance (L3), Objection Handling (L2–L3), Meeting Handoff (L3), Data Hygiene & CRM Discipline (L2)
Managers	Coaching Mastery (L3–L4), Pipeline Inspection & Forecasting (L3–L4), Talent Development (L3), Change Leadership (L2–L3)
Customer Success Managers (CSMs)	Adoption Orchestration (L3), Value Realization Storytelling (L3), Renewal & Expansion Motions (L2–L3), Executive Stakeholder Mangement (L2–L3)

These maps form the foundation for hiring, onboarding, development plans, and promotion criteria.

Coaching is the Execution Engine

Training gives reps exposure. **Coaching drives skills mastery.** Coaching is the structured process of observing demonstrated skills in live or simulated settings and delivering targeted feedback that helps close gaps and reinforce strengths. It creates a safe practice environment where reps can experiment, make mistakes, and immediately refine their approach. When done well, coaching builds confidence, accelerates behavior change, and helps reps transfer learning from theory into field execution.

A good coaching interaction should answer:

· What specific behavior or skill was observed?

· What did the rep do well?

· Where are the gaps or opportunities for improvement?

· What clear next step is required?

· How will progress be measured and followed up?

Coaching is not a forecast call and not a status update; it is guided practice against clearly defined capabilities. It is the bridge between knowing and consistently doing, and when embedded into the sales rhythm, it becomes one of the most powerful levers for improving both individual performance and overall team results.

For Enablement, this means moving beyond creating training sessions and content libraries to building the systems, tools, and playbooks that allow managers to coach effectively. Enablement must:

· Equip managers with coaching frameworks and practical guides.

· Provide data that reveals where skill gaps exist.

· Train managers themselves in the art of coaching, ensuring consistency and quality.

· Ensure every enablement content asset designed for the front line includes explicit guidance on how managers should coach the topic.

· Create feedback loops so coaching outcomes are measured and tied back to performance metrics.

In short, Enablement's job is to operationalize coaching: making it easier for managers to do it well, reinforcing it as a cultural norm, and ensuring that coaching translates into measurable improvements in seller capability and business results.

Peer-Led and Manager-Led Programs

Top Enablement teams mix coaching sources, creating a balanced ecosystem of development and accountability:

- **Manager-led**: Focused, frequent, tied directly to performance and individualized growth plans. Managers act as multipliers when they consistently coach against defined capabilities.

- **Peer-led**: Communities of practice, call-of-the-month reviews, and "what worked" sessions where reps share experiences. Peer-led sessions create belonging and spread effective tactics, but they must be structured and facilitated to reinforce best practices rather than dilute them.

- **Enablement-led**: Formal programs, simulations, and certifications designed to standardize skills and set a clear bar across the organization. These provide the scaffolding for consistency while leaving room for manager and peer reinforcement.

Peer sharing is powerful, but it has to be curated and tied to your process. Don't let bad habits scale under the guise of "tribal knowledge." Enablement teams should actively curate, highlight, and disseminate the best examples, ensuring that peer contributions align with the broader sales methodology and customer engagement model.

Measuring Skills, Not Just Outputs

Knowledge checks are insufficient. Organizations must measure the behaviors that drive outcomes, not just what reps know, but how they actually execute in the field. These measurements should be directly linked back to the capabilities and underlying skills defined earlier. For example, Enablement can instrument coaching and training programs with clear behavioral metrics such as:

- **Talk ratios** and topic coverage in customer conversations, connected to Discovery & Qualification skills.

- **Stage dwell times** and stage-to-stage conversion rates, reflecting proficiency in Opportunity Management capabilities.

- **Usage of sales plays and content assets**, tied to skills like Value Articulation.

- **Correlation between skill proficiency and business results** (e.g., Business Acumen or Discovery capability vs. Stage 2→3 conversion).

When Enablement tracks these behaviors against the defined capabilities, it shifts the conversation from activity for activity's sake to true performance impact. It allows leaders to see which coaching and enablement investments are moving the needle, which capabilities are most predictive of success, and where gaps remain. These metrics ensure development is tied to revenue impact, not activity, making skill building both measurable and strategically relevant.

To make this connection more tangible, here's an example table showing how behavioral metrics can be mapped directly to the **Business Acumen** capability and its underpinning skills defined earlier:

Skill	Example Behavioral Metric	What It Reveals
Business functional knowledge	Percentage of discovery calls where reps ask about the customer's business model, functions, and decision-making process	Depth of understanding of how customer organizations operate
Industry, market & competitor knowledge	Number of deals where reps reference industry trends or competitive positioning during engagement	Ability to contextualize solutions within broader market forces
Company's products & services knowledge	Frequency and quality of tailored value propositions presented to different personas	Skill in connecting product capabilities to customer-specific needs

This mapping illustrates how Enablement can tie capability frameworks to observable, measurable field behaviors, creating a closed loop from **skills definition → execution → measurement → improvement**.

Building a Culture of Coaching

The real unlock is when coaching isn't an initiative but a habit embedded in the company's cultural DNA. When organizations normalize coaching into the daily operating rhythm, it ceases to feel like a program and instead becomes the way business is done.

That requires:

- **Leadership role modeling**: VPs should coach managers, not just inspect forecasts. Senior leaders must demonstrate that coaching is a top priority by investing their own time in it.

- **Recognition systems**: Celebrate coachable moments, not just wins. Highlighting great coaching behaviors in all-hands meetings or newsletters reinforces that capability building is valued as much as bookings.

- **Embedded tooling**: Coaching should happen inside the systems reps already use. Integrating prompts, scorecards, and guided workflows into CRM and conversation intelligence platforms ensures that coaching isn't extra work, but part of the workflow.

- **Manager accountability**: Coaching quality should be part of manager scorecards. Just as managers are held accountable for forecast accuracy, they should also be measured on how effectively they develop their people.

Enablement's role is to help build these cultural and structural reinforcements. This means partnering with leadership to hardwire coaching into performance reviews, designing recognition programs that elevate skill development stories, and working with operations to embed coaching workflows into everyday tools.

Culture eats policy. If you want coaching to stick, make it part of how success is defined, and make Enablement the function that ensures it is operationalized and measured.

Wrap-Up: Grow Sellers, Grow Revenue

You can't scale execution without scaling skill. Coaching is the multiplier that converts onboarding into performance, strategy into behavior, and managers into true leaders. The organizations that win are the ones that make skills development measurable, coaching habitual, and Enablement a catalyst for turning capability frameworks into execution at scale.

Enablement's task is not only to deliver training but to operationalize the system that ensures every role is equipped, every manager is enabled to coach, and every capability is linked to outcomes. When that happens, you don't just grow individual sellers; you grow predictable, repeatable revenue.

A good illustration comes from a global SaaS company that built its sales academy around capability frameworks. Every new program included a manager coaching guide, field metrics were tied back to defined skills, and leadership reinforced coaching as a cultural expectation. Within 12 months, they saw stage-to-stage conversion rates improve by double digits and a measurable uplift in rep productivity. The key wasn't more training hours; it was embedding coaching into the operating system of the business.

The lesson: when Enablement designs for culture, capability, and measurement together, coaching becomes the engine of transformation. Organizations shift from episodic training to a true capability-building system that compounds over time.

Next up: **Activating Sales Plays and Content**, because knowing what to say, when to say it, and having the assets to support it is what transforms skill into action at the point of sale.

Chapter 18: Sales Plays and Field Activation

"Don't just train reps, arm them."

Reps don't need more content. They need the **right content, at the right time, mapped to the right play**. Sales Enablement isn't about producing assets; it's about activating behaviors and creating consistent impact in the field. That activation happens through well-designed sales plays: targeted motions that translate strategy into execution and give reps the confidence to act.

The challenge isn't producing content. It's activating it, embedding it into daily selling rhythms, and ensuring managers reinforce its use. This chapter focuses on how to design, deliver, and operationalize sales plays and content so they actually drive revenue, not just sit in a content portal. We'll explore what makes a play effective, how to align it with GTM strategy, and how to measure whether it truly influences outcomes.

What Is a Sales Play?

A sales play is not a script. It's a **repeatable selling motion** designed to create clarity and consistency in how reps approach specific opportunities. A well-constructed play does more than provide talking points; it equips the rep to recognize the right trigger, engage the right persona, and guide the buyer toward the desired outcome with confidence.

A sales play should:

· Target a specific audience with precision

· Solve a known and validated problem

· Drive a clearly defined outcome tied to business goals

· Use aligned assets, messaging, and proof points

· Provide measurable checkpoints so managers can inspect and coach around it

A good play includes:

- **Trigger**: When and why to run it (e.g., competitor mentioned, new product release, contract renewal approaching)

- **Target**: Who the play is for, segmented by role, industry, or account type

- **Talk Track**: What to say, including open-ended discovery questions and positioning statements

- **Tools**: What to use (i.e., decks, templates, ROI calculators, success stories, or integration guides)

- **CTA**: What action you want the buyer to take, from booking a workshop to engaging in a proof of concept

- **Manager Coaching Guidance**: How frontline leaders should inspect usage and reinforce behaviors in actual customer interactions, 1:1s or deal reviews

If it's not actionable, repeatable, and measurable, it's not a play. Plays must be designed to live inside the operating cadence, ready for activation at scale.

Aligning Plays to GTM Strategy

Your sales plays should be directly mapped to the core pillars of your GTM strategy. Each play should not exist in isolation but act as the bridge that connects high-level plans to day-to-day execution. Mapping ensures clarity for reps and creates consistency across teams.

- **Market segmentation**: Plays should match the specific segments where you've chosen to compete and win.

- **ICP pain points**: Each play must be anchored in the validated pains of your ideal customers, ensuring relevance and urgency.

- **Product positioning**: Align the messaging and assets in the play to how your product uniquely addresses those pains.

- **Campaign calendars**: Integrate plays with Marketing activities so that reps ride the wave of demand creation rather than operating in silos.

- **Sales process stages**: Define which plays best apply at which stage of the process to create a sense of timing and progression.

Examples:

- **"Land and Expand in Manufacturing"** → Target: existing mid-market accounts in industrials. Anchored in expansion strategy, supported by tailored ROI calculators and industry references.

- **"Executive Re-engagement"** → Target: stalled deals at stage 3 with no VP contact. Triggered by lack of senior-level engagement, supported by executive briefing decks.

- **"New Release Launch"** → Target: install base, post-upgrade. Integrated with Marketing launch campaign, paired with demo environments and customer success stories.

Plays are how strategy shows up in the field. They must be **visible, simple to use, and clearly tied to business priorities**. If reps aren't using your plays, they're not executing your strategy, and leadership has lost the most practical lever for aligning daily activity with GTM intent.

Operationalizing Content That Converts

Reps don't have time to sift through 500 PDFs or wonder which version of a deck to use. Content must be curated, streamlined, and surfaced at the exact moment of need. To achieve this, content must be:

- **Role-specific** so that each internal persona (rep, manager, solution consultant, field engineer) finds what is most relevant to them.

- **Deal-stage specific** so the asset maps clearly to the progression of an opportunity and removes guesswork.

- **Easy to find and use** in real time through search, tags, and contextual prompts inside CRM or engagement platforms.

- **Aligned to the buyer's journey**, showing the rep how to advance a prospect from awareness to decision.

Create a **content matrix** that maps buyer journey stages, personas, assets, and CTAs:

Stage	Persona	Asset	CTA
Discover	VP Ops	Industry Trends Deck	Set follow-up workshop
Evaluate	IT	Integration One-Pager	Schedule technical validation
Decision	CFO	ROI Calculator	Gain budget approval
Adoption	End User	Quick Start Guide	Drive product usage and feedback
Expansion	Business Unit Lead	Case Study on Expansion	Identify cross-sell opportunity

Beyond building the matrix, organizations must **tag, govern, and retire** content. Tag content accordingly in your enablement platform or CRM. Establish ownership so assets remain current, and create retirement workflows to remove outdated materials. This prevents clutter, drives higher adoption, and ensures reps always have confidence they are using the most accurate and compelling content.

Activation Tactics That Work

It's not enough to launch a play. You have to drive adoption, embed it into the team's routines, and make it part of how business gets done. Plays must be reinforced consistently, not treated as one-off campaigns. Adoption tactics include:

- **Call Blitzes**: Live call sessions focused on one play. These create energy, accountability, and immediate proof of concept.

- **Team Roleplays**: Practice talk tracks with manager feedback. Repetition builds confidence and exposes gaps before reps face buyers.

- **Deal Reviews**: Inspect live opps using the play. Managers and peers can reinforce which parts of the play are being applied and where adjustments are needed.

- **Manager Scorecards**: Track rep usage and effectiveness. Scorecards create visibility and give leaders tangible ways to recognize progress and address gaps.

- **Field Champions**: Peer-led enablement from top performers. Champions serve as multipliers, showing others how to apply the play in real deals.

· **Micro-Coaching Moments**: Encourage managers to weave play-specific feedback into daily 1:1s, forecast calls, and pipeline inspections.

· **Celebrations and Recognition**: Highlight wins that result from plays in team meetings or company comms to reinforce adoption.

Plays must become part of the **operating cadence**, woven into reviews, coaching, and deal strategy discussions. Only then do they truly shift behavior at scale.

To help teams visualize this integration, create an **activation calendar** that sequences enablement tactics across a quarter.

Week	Tactic	Objective
Week 1	Play Launch Workshop	Introduce objectives, triggers, and talk tracks
Week 2	Call Blitz	Drive immediate application and quick wins
Week 3	Team Roleplay	Reinforce messaging and practice objection handling
Week 4	Deal Reviews	Inspect application in live opportunities
Week 5	Recognition & Sharing	Highlight wins, share peer success stories
Week 6	Micro-Coaching	Managers weave play feedback into 1:1s
Week 7	Peer Champion Spotlight	Showcase top rep usage of the play
Week 8	Manager Scorecard Review	Measure adoption, impact, and areas for reinforcement
Week 9	Refresher Training	Address gaps surfaced in data or feedback
Week 10	Expanded Call Blitz	Extend adoption across broader teams
Week 11	Advanced Roleplays	Focus on complex scenarios or executive conversations
Week 12	Play Effectiveness Review	Evaluate metrics, retire or scale the play

This rolling calendar ensures that no play is a one-and-done event. It becomes part of the operating rhythm, reinforced through repetition, inspection, coaching, and recognition. Over time, this creates the muscle memory needed for consistent execution at scale.

Measuring Play Effectiveness

Every play should have metrics to ensure they are not just launched but are actually driving value in the field. These metrics must be quantitative and qualitative, giving leaders and reps alike a full picture of effectiveness.

- **Adoption**: Who's using it? Look at both breadth (how many reps) and depth (how consistently they apply it).

- **Activation**: How often is it used in real deals? Track frequency of play usage tied to opportunity stages.

- **Influence**: What impact is it having on win rate, cycle time, and ASP? This connects enablement efforts directly to business outcomes.

- **Feedback**: What reps and buyers are saying. Capture structured rep feedback as well as customer sentiment from surveys or deal retros.

Organizations should review these data points regularly, ideally as part of quarterly business reviews. Plays that underperform should be killed or revised quickly, while top performers should be highlighted, celebrated, and scaled across the field. This creates a **dynamic portfolio**, not a static library; one that evolves based on evidence, stays relevant to changing market conditions, and builds trust that Enablement isn't just producing noise but delivering impact.

To make these insights tangible, build a **Play Performance Dashboard** that visualizes adoption, activation, influence, and feedback in one place.

Metric	Visualization	Insight Provided
Adoption	% of reps actively using play	Shows breadth and depth of field usage
Activation	# of opportunities with play tag	Reveals frequency and consistency of real-world use
Influence	Win rate, ASP, cycle time vs. avg	Connects enablement to direct business outcomes
Feedback	Rep NPS, buyer sentiment highlights	Captures qualitative signals and improvement requests

Dashboards should be embedded in the CRM or enablement platform so leaders can inspect performance during QBRs and managers can reference in weekly coaching sessions. Visualizing performance turns Enablement into a measurable, data-driven function; closing the loop between play design, field execution, and revenue impact.

Marketing and Enablement Partnership

Content without context doesn't move deals. Content strategy must be a cross-functional effort that unites Marketing, Product Marketing, field teams, and Enablement. Without alignment, assets risk becoming disconnected noise rather than catalysts for buyer engagement.

Ensure that:

· Marketing aligns campaign content with sales play objectives and ensures timing supports active field priorities.

· Product Marketing provides messaging **aligned to personas and pain**, not just features, and updates it consistently as markets and competitors shift.

· Field feedback loops back into content strategy through structured capture mechanisms (deal reviews, surveys, win/loss analysis) so assets continuously evolve.

· Leadership reinforces the expectation that every new piece of content or play must include coaching guidance for managers, so activation is supported at all levels.

Enablement should own the activation layer -where content meets behavior- curating, sequencing, and embedding it into operating rhythms. By acting as the bridge between strategy and execution, Enablement ensures that content is not only produced but applied in the field to influence outcomes.

Case in Point: One enterprise SaaS company launched a new solution with extensive Marketing materials but failed to integrate them into sales plays. Reps defaulted to old decks, messaging was inconsistent, and buyers received conflicting stories. Pipeline stalled, and leadership blamed rep execution. After revisiting the enablement approach, the company restructured content into targeted plays, aligned assets to buyer roles, and equipped managers with coaching guides. Within two quarters, play adoption rose above 70%, win rates improved by 12%, and leadership gained confidence that field execution matched strategy.

This contrast highlights why alignment, ownership, and coaching guidance are non-negotiables for effective sales content and play activation.

Cross-Industry Perspectives: The same principle applies beyond SaaS. In industrial manufacturing, for example, one company introduced a complex automation solution without integrating field enablement. Sellers struggled to articulate ROI in plant-level terms, slowing adoption. Once Enablement created a play with tailored ROI calculators and industry case studies, adoption spiked and deals accelerated. In HR tech, a provider rolled out new compliance tools but failed to equip managers with coaching guides. Reps reverted to generic messaging until Enablement rewired plays to align with CHRO and HRBP personas, doubling engagement in executive conversations.

These examples show that regardless of industry, content activation through plays and coaching makes the difference between noise and measurable impact.

RevOps and Enablement Partnership

RevOps and Enablement are natural allies in making sales plays stick. Each brings complementary strengths: RevOps provides the data, process discipline, and systems integration, while Enablement ensures those insights translate into frontline behaviors and coaching. Together, they turn strategy into repeatable execution.

- **RevOps Contributions**: Design tagging in CRM to track play usage, build dashboards that measure adoption and impact, and surface insights on which plays drive pipeline velocity and conversion improvements.

- **Enablement Contributions**: Create the plays, curate the content, train the field, and equip managers with coaching guides. Enablement translates RevOps insights into actionable training and reinforcement.

- **Joint Accountability**: Meet regularly to review play performance data, retire underperforming assets, and co-design the next generation of plays based on field feedback and revenue metrics.

· **Impact**: When RevOps and Enablement operate in lockstep, sellers know exactly what to use, managers know how to coach it, and leadership can see clear evidence of impact on revenue outcomes.

This partnership ensures that sales plays are not just well-designed but also measurable, adaptable, and embedded in the operating rhythm of the business.

Example in Practice: At a global HR tech provider, RevOps noticed through CRM tagging that adoption of a new "Compliance Play" was lagging. Enablement partnered with RevOps to diagnose the issue: data revealed managers weren't coaching to the play, and reps defaulted to generic messaging. In response, RevOps simplified the tagging process and built a dashboard showing play usage at the deal level. Enablement then delivered manager coaching sessions and provided frontline leaders with scorecards. Within one quarter, adoption jumped from 25% to 75%, and the influenced pipeline grew by 18%. This collaboration demonstrated how RevOps insights plus Enablement activation creates measurable impact.

Wrap-Up: Equip to Execute

Great strategy without great execution is just theory. Sales plays and content are the vehicles that bring GTM strategy to life at scale, across teams, and in live deals. But success requires more than building a playbook. Plays must be aligned to strategy, reinforced by managers, measured with discipline, and continuously improved through feedback and data.

Enablement and RevOps together ensure that content is contextualized, activated, and visible in the operating cadence. Marketing and product teams contribute by anchoring messaging in buyer pain, while managers coach consistently so that plays become muscle memory in the field. This collective effort transforms content from static assets into repeatable behaviors that drive measurable outcomes.

The call to action: **design plays that matter, operationalize them through adoption tactics, track their impact with dashboards, and evolve them as markets change.** Done right, plays and content become the connective tissue between strategy and execution.

From here, we turn to another critical dimension of the Revenue Enablement pillar: **Sales Manager Enablement**, covering how to equip frontline leaders to coach effectively, enforce discipline, and multiply the impact of every enablement initiative.

Chapter 19: Sales Manager Enablement

"Managers are the multipliers of performance."

As established in *Chapter 14: Sales Manager as Execution Multiplier*, managers are the ultimate force multipliers for enablement. Yet most organizations underinvest in equipping them, assuming top sellers will automatically become strong leaders. The outcome: weak coaching, poor pipeline discipline, and missed targets.

This chapter focuses on the key components of a structured **sales manager enablement program**, with a special emphasis on **manager onboarding** and **continuous development**.

Manager Onboarding

New managers face a steep learning curve. Manager onboarding should focus squarely on the **core activities that define effective frontline sales leadership**: inspecting, coaching, and holding people accountable for performance.

- **Inspection**: Teach managers how to ensure their teams are doing what they are supposed to. This includes running disciplined pipeline reviews, deal inspections, and forecast calls, but also checking what their reps are spending their time on. They must learn to separate activity from progress and to identify early signals of risk.

- **Coaching**: Enable managers to help their teams do what they are doing even better. Provide frameworks and roleplays to practice observing rep behaviors and delivering actionable feedback. New managers should master running structured 1:1s and in-the-moment call coaching sessions.

- **Accountability**: Train managers on setting clear expectations, tracking commitments, and addressing underperformance quickly and constructively.

Manager onboarding must also instill mastery of the **cadences and rhythms** that drive consistency:

- Weekly 1:1s with reps that blend performance-to-quota reviews, deal coaching and skill development.

- Weekly pipeline inspections and forecast reviews.

- Monthly team performance reviews tied to both results and behaviors.

- Quarterly business reviews that connect team outcomes to company goals.

Role-specific simulations (e.g., leading a forecast call, conducting a coaching session) and pairing with experienced mentors help accelerate confidence and capability.

The goal is not just to orient managers to policies, but to build leaders who can reliably inspect, coach, and enforce accountability within consistent operating rhythms, thus reducing the time it takes to lead effectively and deliver consistent team results.

Continuous Manager Development

Enablement should not stop after onboarding. Continuous development is where good managers evolve into great leaders. It ensures they don't plateau after the first six months but continue to sharpen the core skills that sustain team performance.

- **Coaching Mastery**: Managers need structured refreshers and practice in observing skills, delivering targeted feedback, and tracking behavioral change. This should include advanced modules on differentiating between deal inspection and true skill coaching.

- **Pipeline & Forecasting Excellence**: Beyond initial training, managers should attend recurring workshops on forecasting accuracy, deal inspection, and leading indicators. Use case studies from their own pipelines to make learning immediately applicable.

- **Talent Development**: Equip managers with guidance on hiring profiles, structured interview practices, onboarding best practices, and succession planning. Continuous development here ensures managers are always thinking about building tomorrow's team, not just managing today's.

- **Leadership Skills**: Expand training into areas like strategic communication, running effective team meetings, conflict resolution, and leading through change. Managers must be able to motivate, align, and guide their teams in both stable and turbulent markets.

Continuous development should follow clear cadences too: quarterly manager enablement sessions, bi-annual certifications, and monthly peer forums where managers exchange best practices and challenges. By embedding development into rhythms, organizations reinforce the message that manager growth is as non-negotiable as revenue growth.

Tools and Support

Provide managers with practical resources that make their core activities -inspecting, coaching, and holding teams accountable- easier and more consistent:

- **Standardized 1:1 templates** for coaching and performance reviews, ensuring conversations are structured and outcome-oriented.

- **Pipeline inspection guides** tied to sales stages, helping managers know exactly what to look for in deal reviews and how to separate real progress from activity noise.

- **Call review scorecards** that provide a common framework for feedback, making coaching repeatable and less subjective.

- **Dashboards** that connect team performance metrics with enablement initiatives, giving managers visibility into how behaviors and enablement programs impact outcomes.

- **Operating rhythm playbooks** that outline weekly, monthly, and quarterly cadences, ensuring managers keep a consistent drumbeat across inspection, coaching, and accountability.

- **Call planning frameworks** that help managers prepare with reps for upcoming customer interactions, ensuring each meeting has a clear objective, anticipated objections, tailored messaging, and defined next steps.

- **Forecasting call guides** that equip managers to run disciplined forecast calls, align expectations with leadership, and coach reps on improving forecast accuracy.

- **Deal review frameworks** that standardize how managers inspect live opportunities, focus on stage-appropriate behaviors, and coach reps to improve deal strategy and execution.

These resources not only save managers time but also embed best practices into daily operations, reinforcing the rhythms that drive high performance.

Partnership with Enablement and RevOps

Before exploring the roles of Enablement, RevOps, and frontline managers, it's important to understand that manager enablement is not a solo function. It is a **shared system of support** in which each group contributes distinct value but relies on the others to succeed. When these parts work together, managers gain the clarity, tools, and insight they need to lead consistently and effectively.

- **RevOps** delivers actionable insights (conversion rates, coverage, forecast accuracy) that give managers visibility into where their teams are excelling and where risks are emerging. These insights should be translated into specific coaching themes, prioritized based on impact.

- **Enablement** supplies structured playbooks, coaching programs, and ongoing reinforcement, but its role goes beyond distributing materials. Enablement should actively partner with managers to ensure that every playbook and training is embedded into daily rhythms and linked back to outcomes.

- **Managers** then translate these inputs into targeted coaching for their teams, using enablement frameworks and RevOps data to guide 1:1s, team sessions, and call planning. In practice, this means turning raw numbers into behaviors -i.e. if conversion rates dip at discovery, managers know to focus coaching on questioning skills and qualification discipline-.

Measuring Manager Enablement Impact

Assess whether manager enablement is working by tracking a balanced set of outcome and behavior metrics. Effectiveness isn't only about results; it's about how broadly and consistently managers participate in the rhythms of enablement and how many of their reps achieve success. To evaluate these factors effectively, organizations should look at metrics such as:

· Rep ramp speed by manager.

· Overall quota attainment variance across sales teams.

· Breadth of quota attainment participation across teams (% of reps hitting quota under a manager).

· Coaching quality scores and rep feedback.

· Retention and engagement of high-performing reps.

· Adoption and quality of execution of core cadences (percentage of 1:1s completed, pipeline reviews held, call coaching sessions conducted).

By combining outcome and behavioral data, organizations get a holistic view: not only which managers deliver short-term results, but which ones create sustainable, scalable performance systems that consistently lift the entire team.

Wrap-Up: Building Scalable Leadership

Sales manager enablement is not optional, it's the linchpin of scalable performance. Managers are the ones who translate enablement programs into daily execution, ensuring strategies become lived behaviors in the field. By investing in structured onboarding, continuous development, and equipping managers with the right tools, organizations create leaders who can inspect rigorously, coach effectively, and hold teams accountable. This turns managers into true multipliers of performance: amplifying every enablement initiative, sustaining cultural consistency, and ensuring execution scales with growth.

From here, we turn to the next critical topic in the Revenue Enablement pillar: Measurement and Feedback Loops, discussing how to track impact, gather insights, and use data to continuously refine enablement programs so they remain outcome-focused and business-driven.

Chapter 20: Measurement & Feedback Loops

"What gets measured gets improved."

Enablement must be treated like any other revenue-critical function: it thrives when tied to clear metrics and continuous feedback. Without measurement, Enablement risks being seen as a cost center rather than a growth driver. In practice, this means defining success upfront, tracking both leading and lagging indicators, and embedding structured listening from the field. Beyond simply proving ROI, measurement and feedback create a learning system where programs evolve with the business. This chapter explores how to build measurement and feedback systems that make Enablement accountable, adaptive, and outcome-focused, ensuring it is seen as a strategic growth lever rather than a discretionary expense.

Why Measurement Matters

Measurement transforms Enablement from a series of activities into a business driver. By linking programs to leading indicators such as time-to-first deal, stage conversion rates, play adoption, and coaching quality, organizations can prove the ROI of Enablement and refine approaches in real time.

This shift reframes Enablement as more than training delivery; it becomes a performance system. For example, shortening time-to-first deal shows that onboarding is not only efficient but revenue-producing. Tracking stage conversions reveals whether reps are translating learning into effective deal execution. Play adoption signals cultural alignment and consistency, while coaching quality highlights whether managers are multiplying Enablement's impact. When these data points are reviewed consistently with leadership, they guide decisions on where to invest, what to adjust, and which programs to scale. In other words, measurement connects Enablement directly to business outcomes and builds the credibility needed to secure ongoing investment.

Core Metrics for Enablement

Here are the core measures that bring Enablement's impact into focus, spanning onboarding, deal execution, manager coaching, and ultimate revenue outcomes:

- **Breadth of Participation**: The percentage of reps consistently hitting or exceeding quota. This is the most holistic KPI, reflecting Enablement's mission to maximize the number of sellers who succeed.

- **Time-to-First Deal**: How quickly new hires close their first deal. An indicator of onboarding effectiveness.

- **Stage Conversion Rates**: Movement of opportunities through the funnel, showing whether reps are applying enablement in real deals.

- **Play Adoption**: Percentage of reps using plays, measured by CRM tagging or activity tracking.

- **Coaching Quality**: Manager-led coaching effectiveness, measured via scorecards, rep surveys, and/or call review assessments.

- **Win Rates & Average Selling Price (ASP)**: Outcome metrics tied directly to revenue impact.

- **Competency / Skill Data Correlation**: Mapping rep skill proficiency against performance outcomes, highlighting which capabilities drive quota attainment and where targeted enablement can close gaps.

Feedback Loops

Numbers alone aren't enough. Effective enablement requires feedback loops that connect the field to the function and ensure the voice of every stakeholder is heard and acted upon:

- **Rep Feedback**: Gather insights on what's useful, missing, or outdated. Examples include pulse surveys after training, focus groups, or open feedback channels tied to specific plays.

- **Manager Feedback**: Capture whether managers can coach and reinforce enablement in daily rhythms. This should include structured scorecards from 1:1 coaching sessions and observations from deal reviews.

· **Customer Feedback**: Use win/loss analysis and post-sale surveys to understand how enablement messaging lands with buyers. Pair this with buyer verbatims to identify gaps in positioning or proof points.

· **Cross-Functional Feedback**: Include Marketing, Product, and RevOps perspectives to spot misalignments and ensure Enablement efforts support broader GTM motions.

Feedback must be structured and continuous, not ad hoc. Embed surveys, deal retros, and QBR debriefs as part of the operating rhythm. Over time, these loops create a culture where enablement is shaped by real-world usage and continuously adapts to market dynamics.

Closing the Loop

The goal is not just to measure but to act. Enablement teams must regularly review metrics and feedback with RevOps and Sales Leadership, retire what doesn't work, and double down on what does.

This requires a disciplined cadence: monthly reviews for tactical adjustments, quarterly reviews for program redesign, and annual reviews to align with strategic goals. Dashboards should make progress visible at every level -reps, managers, and executives- so that enablement outcomes are transparent and action-oriented.

When leaders and reps alike can see progress in black and white, trust grows in the system, adoption accelerates, and Enablement earns a permanent seat at the growth table.

Wrap-Up: From Cost Center to Growth Driver

Measurement and feedback loops elevate Enablement from a support function to a strategic engine of growth. The breadth of participation metric shows whether more sellers are consistently winning. Leading indicators like time-to-first deal and stage conversion rates reveal where learning translates into execution, while lagging metrics such as win rates and ASP prove ultimate business impact.

Feedback loops ensure these insights aren't static but continuously shape programs that stay relevant. Together, measurement and feedback create a virtuous cycle; one that makes Enablement accountable, adaptive, and indispensable.

When embedded in the GTM operating rhythm, Enablement is no longer seen as overhead but recognized as a multiplier of execution and a driver of scalable growth.

In the next chapter, we'll cover the final piece of the Revenue Enablement pillar: **Tech-Enabled Learning and Performance Support** and how to embed enablement into the daily flow of work with the help of AI and modern tools.

Chapter 21: Tech-Enabled Learning and Performance Support

"Reps don't need more training. They need better support... In the moment, not the month."

Traditional training is too slow for modern sales. Reps forget most of what they hear in onboarding within weeks, and without reinforcement, new knowledge rarely changes field behavior. Content portals often get ignored because they are disconnected from day-to-day selling. And playbooks that live in static slide decks are quickly outdated and seldom reopened once the launch moment has passed.

Today's high-performing GTM organizations are shifting from **event-based enablement** to **embedded enablement**, where learning and support happen in the flow of work, triggered by live selling moments and aligned to buyer conversations. This shift recognizes that reps need guidance at the exact point of execution, not weeks or months later.

This chapter explores how technology, especially AI, is transforming Enablement from a reactive, back-office function into a real-time performance layer that amplifies rep effectiveness, equips managers with actionable insights, and ensures organizations continuously translate strategy into front-line execution.

From One-Time Training to Continuous Enablement

Reps don't need a one-time download of product knowledge. They need ongoing, contextual support that reinforces behaviors and builds confidence in the field. They need:

· **Ongoing reinforcement of key behaviors** through micro-learnings and manager-led coaching moments

· **Contextual reminders** tied to deal stage or buyer role, surfaced automatically inside the CRM or engagement platform

- **Quick access** to battle cards, proof points, or objection handling tools that are always current and role-relevant

- **Micro-coaching** based on what's actually happening in their pipeline, informed by data from call recordings, forecast reviews, or buyer interactions

- **Personalized nudges** and adaptive learning paths driven by AI, ensuring each rep gets exactly what they need based on performance and upcoming opportunities

Modern enablement is **persistent, personalized, and performance-driven**, designed to meet the rep at the moment of need, not just in the classroom.

Example in Action: Imagine a rep preparing for a late-stage CFO meeting. As soon as they open the opportunity in CRM, an AI assistant surfaces a one-page ROI calculator, recent competitive intel, and a recommended talk track for financial executives. During the meeting, the conversational intelligence tool listens and prompts with objection-handling cues when the CFO questions implementation costs. After the call, the system generates a coaching summary for the manager, highlighting where the rep excelled and where reinforcement is needed. The next day, the rep receives a micro-learning module focused on handling cost-based objections, reinforcing exactly what they encountered in the live deal.

This scenario illustrates how embedded enablement works: guidance at the point of need, real-time coaching support, and personalized reinforcement that drives confidence and consistency in execution.

The Tech Stack That Enables the Field

A best-in-class enablement stack includes not just a list of technologies, but an ecosystem designed to work together in the flow of work. Key components include:

- **Learning Management System (LMS) or Learning Experience Platform (LXP)** for structured learning paths, certifications, and ongoing reinforcement. These should adapt to role, region, and product focus.

- **Sales Enablement Platform (SEP)** for delivering content, tracking usage, and surfacing analytics on what actually drives deal progression.

- **Conversational Intelligence** tools for call recording, transcription, and AI-driven analysis that highlight patterns, coaching opportunities, and competitive trends.

- **Digital Sales Rooms** or Deal Portals to co-create value with buyers, centralizing proposals, case studies, and collaborative resources in one secure place.

- **AI Assistants** for real-time guidance, surfacing the right content or messaging suggestion based on buyer role, deal stage, or objection in the moment.

- **Analytics & RevOps Dashboards** that tie enablement activity to pipeline metrics, conversion rates, and revenue outcomes.

The power of the stack lies in integration. These tools should embed seamlessly into CRM and sales engagement platforms, not live as standalone islands. When connected, they create a unified enablement experience where insights flow to managers, guidance flows to reps, and data flows back to leadership.

To clarify the value of each tool, map them to the distinct needs of **reps, managers, and leadership** in a simple table:

Tool	Value for Reps	Value for Managers	Value for Leadership
LMS / LXP	Bite-sized learning, role-based certifications	Visibility into rep progress, skill gaps	Proof of readiness across regions and roles
Sales Enablement Platform	Easy access to assets in context	Data on asset usage and coaching opportunities	Evidence of content ROI, alignment with GTM goals
Conversational Intelligence	Real-time call insights and self-coaching	Objective coaching data, trend spotting	Aggregate insights on messaging and market signals
Digital Sales Rooms	Seamless buyer collaboration, single source of truth	Visibility into buyer engagement and decision dynamics	Signals of deal health and forecast accuracy
AI Assistants	Contextual prompts and objection handling	Reinforcement cues to support coaching in the moment	Efficiency gains and consistent message delivery

| Analytics & RevOps Dashboards | Clear link between actions and outcomes | Manager-level scorecards, inspection data | Enterprise-level performance insights |

Phasing Technology Adoption

Rolling out a full enablement stack all at once can overwhelm the field and dilute adoption. Instead, organizations should phase their investments and activation in a deliberate sequence:

1. **Foundation First:** Start with the LMS/LXP to establish structured learning and certification. Pair it with a sales enablement platform to centralize content and ensure consistency.

2. **Add Real-Time Insights:** Once content and learning foundations are in place, layer on conversational intelligence and AI assistants to provide live feedback and guidance.

3. **Enable Buyer Collaboration:** Introduce digital sales rooms when the field demonstrates maturity with internal tools, allowing external engagement to be streamlined and tracked.

4. **Scale with Analytics:** Finally, connect everything through RevOps dashboards to measure impact across adoption, conversion, and revenue.

This phased approach avoids tool fatigue, builds trust in the stack, and ensures every layer is adopted before adding the next. Leaders should revisit adoption quarterly to decide when the field is ready for the next stage.

Just-in-Time Enablement: Delivering When It Matters

The key to adoption is timing and relevance. Tools and content must be **delivered in the flow of work**, not buried in portals or delayed until after the fact. Deliver:

· **Objection responses** surfaced during live calls (via AI or call plugins), ensuring reps feel confident addressing buyer concerns in the moment.

174

- **Playbooks and talk tracks** linked to CRM opportunity stage, so guidance feels natural and contextual rather than generic.

- **Customer stories and proof points** filtered by industry, persona, and use case, giving reps credibility with examples buyers actually relate to.

- **Competitor insights** that pop when a rival's name is mentioned, equipping reps with proactive counters instead of reactive scrambling.

- **Manager coaching prompts** aligned to these same triggers, so leaders can reinforce best practices in 1:1s or deal reviews.

When the right tool or insight shows up exactly when the rep needs it, adoption follows naturally. If it doesn't, it becomes clutter and collects digital dust.

Leveraging AI for Coaching and Personalization

AI isn't replacing Enablement... It's **supercharging** it. But as we explored earlier in *Chapter 15: Strategic Enablement*, technology alone is not the differentiator. Knowledge is now table stakes; what matters is context, judgment, and true business acumen. AI can automate tasks, generate content, and surface insights at scale, but it cannot replace the critical thinking, coaching, and customer-centric perspective that Enablement must build.

Use AI to:

- **Analyze call recordings** for talk track adherence, objection handling, and engagement patterns

- **Generate personalized learning paths** based on rep performance data

- **Recommend micro-learnings** based on upcoming meetings or deal stage

- **Summarize long-form content** into role-specific key points

- **Flag pipeline risk** based on missed discovery questions or silence after pricing

When combined with Enablement's role of teaching reps how to think, equipping managers to coach for decision quality, and embedding outcome-focused judgment across the GTM org, AI becomes a force multiplier. It enables scale without sacrificing relevance, while Enablement ensures the strategic muscle behind the technology is strong.

Field Usage and Feedback Loops

Tools don't matter if they're not used. Build feedback loops that go beyond counting clicks and logins; they must link adoption to impact and continuously inform program design. For example, if certain assets drive higher conversion rates in one segment but fall flat in another, that insight should trigger content tailoring, coaching reinforcement, or even strategic pivots. Reps and managers should be part of this loop, sharing what works in the field and what never makes it off the shelf. Marketing and product teams can feed in signals about shifting buyer priorities or competitive moves, ensuring enablement assets evolve in real time. To make these insights actionable, consider the following practices:

- **Monitor usage of content** by team, region, and segment, looking for adoption patterns and anomalies

- **Tie usage to outcomes** (e.g., does using this asset improve win rates or deal velocity?)

- **Gather rep feedback** on what's missing, confusing, or outdated, and loop those insights back into content design

- **Create content retirement workflows:** less is more, and clutter reduces trust and adoption

The best enablement platforms evolve with the field. They are dynamic, data-driven systems that reflect the realities of the market, ensuring that the right content, tools, and coaching are always aligned to what sellers need in the moment.

Change Management and Adoption Tactics

Even the best tools fail without adoption. That's why change management must be intentional and multi-layered, combining clear use cases, leadership alignment, and reinforcement over time. Tactics that work include:

- **Launch with a use case** (e.g., support for a new sales play) so reps immediately see relevance.

- **Enable the managers first**: they drive rep behavior and become the lever for scaling adoption.

- **Reward usage tied to outcomes**, not just clicks, showing that adoption translates to real performance gains.

- **Create champions** in the field who drive peer adoption by modeling success and sharing stories.

- **Integrate into operating rhythms**, not side channels, embedding the tech into pipeline reviews, forecast calls, and deal coaching.

Adoption requires storytelling, reinforcement, and visible leadership sponsorship. Managers must model the behavior, executives must highlight wins tied to the tools, and reps must experience tangible time savings or deal impact. In short, enablement tech is only as powerful as the change management behind it; and change management succeeds when adoption becomes the natural way of working rather than another initiative to remember.

Wrap-Up: Performance, Not Portals

The future of Enablement is not more training. It's **performance support that shows up when and where it matters**. It's real-time, role-specific, and personalized. And it's enabled by technology that integrates -not disrupts- the seller's workflow.

What we've seen across these chapters is a progression: from defining metrics and feedback loops that prove impact, to embedding technology that delivers enablement in the flow of work, to recognizing that AI raises the bar by making knowledge abundant but judgment scarce. The common thread is that Enablement is shifting from delivering information to building capability, context, and confidence at scale.

A critical part of this is defining and measuring **skill data**. Understanding the specific skills each role requires -how proficient individuals are across the team and how those skill levels correlate with performance-gives leaders clarity on where gaps exist. This data becomes the driver for enablement priorities, ensuring efforts target the most impactful areas and align with business outcomes. Without it, organizations risk investing in content and tools that miss the mark.

This is how Enablement earns its place as a strategic multiplier: by combining measurement with feedback, layering in just-in-time tech support, harnessing AI responsibly to strengthen decision quality, and grounding everything in a clear view of role-specific skill needs. The result is not a library of content, but a performance system that adapts in real time to market conditions and equips every seller to succeed.

That wraps the Revenue Enablement pillar. You've now built a system that not only plans effectively and executes with discipline, but equips your teams to win consistently and at scale.

In the final section, we tie it all together in the **GTM Operating System**, where Planning, Execution, and Enablement operate as one cohesive engine.

Part IV: The GTM Operating System

Chapter 22: Unifying Planning, Execution, and Enablement

"Strategy wins in design. Execution wins in the field. Excellence happens when both speak the same language."

You've built the plan. You're executing with discipline. You've enabled the field. But without integration, even best-in-class functions operate in silos. Planning gets disconnected from reality. Execution becomes rigid or reactive. Enablement loses relevance.

The missing piece in most B2B organizations isn't talent, effort, or tools… It's **orchestration**.

This chapter lays out how to integrate Planning, Execution, and Enablement into a **unified GTM operating system**: one that scales, adapts, and drives performance across the entire revenue engine.

The GTM Disconnect: A Systemic Problem

Here's how GTM breaks down in the real world:

- **Planning** happens in Q4, based on board targets, not market realities. Teams often spend weeks producing elaborate plans that look good in slide decks but don't reflect field feedback or buyer trends. By the time those plans hit the market, conditions have already shifted.

- **Execution** is inspected in Q1, usually after things start slipping. Leaders review lagging indicators, discover pipeline gaps or forecast misses, and scramble to patch holes rather than proactively managing performance.

- **Enablement** is asked to fix it in Q2, with too little context, too late. Training programs or sales plays are rolled out reactively, disconnected from the original planning assumptions or real execution gaps.

By then, the damage is done. Sellers are frustrated by mixed messages, cycles are wasted chasing unwinnable opportunities, and leadership is left scrambling to explain missed revenue targets to the board.

This lag between planning, action, and support creates friction, duplication of effort, wasted spend, and missed growth opportunities. Functions point fingers instead of pulling in the same direction, and trust between the field and headquarters erodes.

You can't fix that with better tools or another dashboard. You need a **connected system**: one where planning is dynamic, execution is inspected in real time, and enablement is proactive, not reactive.

The GTM Operating System Defined

A **GTM Operating System** is the combination of:

- **A shared set of rhythms, workflows, and metrics** that align teams on what matters most and eliminate siloed scorecards.

- **Clear roles and accountability across functions**, ensuring Marketing, Sales, Success, Finance, and Enablement know who owns what and how their work connects to revenue.

- **Real-time feedback loops** that drive iteration, turning data from the field into immediate adjustments in messaging, plays, and coverage.

- **A unified view of performance, execution, and readiness** that ties together leading and lagging indicators into one shared narrative.

Think of the GTM OS like the operating system of a computer: it doesn't replace the applications (Sales, Marketing, Success, Enablement) but provides the environment where they run in harmony, share resources, and adapt to new inputs. Without it, each function operates in isolation; with it, the whole machine runs faster, smoother, and more predictably.

It turns annual planning into continuous execution. It turns enablement into a force multiplier. And it makes GTM leadership a team sport, not a turf war.

Core Components of the GTM OS

1. Integrated Planning Process

RevOps, Finance, Sales, Marketing, and Enablement co-own segmentation, capacity, territory, and campaign alignment.

This means that instead of each function creating its own version of the plan, they sit at the same table to define how the market will be segmented, how much selling capacity is available, how territories will be designed, and how campaigns will align with field coverage.

RevOps brings the data, Finance ensures financial discipline, Sales defines coverage priorities, Marketing aligns demand generation, and Enablement ensures the field has the skills and plays to execute.

The output isn't a static plan but a living blueprint that all functions are accountable to, and that can flex as conditions change.

2. Execution Feedback Loops

Insights from forecast calls, pipeline reviews, win/loss analysis, and observed buyer behavior inform both enablement and planning.

In practice, this means that:

- **Forecast Calls** surface not only deal probabilities but also reveal patterns in objections, common blockers, and cycle length trends.

- **Pipeline Reviews** highlight where opportunities consistently stall, pointing to potential skill gaps, ineffective messaging, or process friction.

- **Win/Loss Analysis** uncovers recurring themes in why deals are won or lost, ranging from pricing dynamics and competitive positioning to buyer experience.

- **Buyer Behavior Signals** track digital engagement, content consumption, and meeting participation, showing where interest is increasing or declining across accounts and segments.

When fed back into Enablement, these insights shape training, sales plays, and messaging.

When fed back into planning, they influence segmentation, coverage, and campaign priorities.

The result is a feedback loop that makes planning proactive and enablement precise.

3. Enablement Embedded in Rhythm

Sales plays, onboarding, and coaching are scheduled in lockstep with the GTM calendar (QBRs, SKO, product launches).

This means Enablement isn't running on its own timeline but is fully integrated into the company's commercial rhythms.

For example:

- **Onboarding Programs**: Refreshed ahead of each SKO to ensure new hires are aligned with the latest strategy, messaging, and plays.

- **Sales Plays**: Launched in sync with product releases, giving reps immediate tools and messaging to bring new offerings to market.

- **Coaching Programs**: Timed with quarterly business reviews so managers can reinforce priorities, sharpen skills, and drive accountability tied to business outcomes.

The result is that Enablement becomes a proactive driver of readiness, embedding learning and reinforcement directly into the operating cadence of the business rather than as ad-hoc activities.

4. Cross-Functional Governance

A GTM Council or Operating Committee **meets monthly** to track alignment, surface blockers, and reallocate resources.

In practice, this looks like a structured 60–90 minute session where cross-functional leaders (Sales, Marketing, Success, Finance, Product, Enablement, and RevOps) come together with one shared scorecard.

The agenda typically covers:

- **Review Progress Against Shared KPIs**: Ensure the organization is tracking toward common objectives, not siloed metrics.

- **Identify Systemic Blockers**: Surface challenges that cross functions and require joint solutions rather than localized fixes.

- **Reallocate Resources**: Shift budget, headcount, or program focus to areas with the highest impact potential.

- **Capture Field Feedback**: Collect insights from reps and managers to feed back into planning and enablement for continuous improvement.

The Council is not a reporting meeting but a decision-making forum designed to keep the GTM engine synchronized and responsive between formal planning cycles.

From a governance perspective, facilitation is typically best owned by **Revenue Operations (RevOps)**, acting as the neutral orchestrator across functions. RevOps ensures the agenda is prepared, the right data and insights are brought into the discussion, and follow-up actions are documented and tracked. This keeps the meeting disciplined, outcome-oriented, and unbiased toward any single function.

5. Single Source of Truth

Dashboards and scorecards tie Planning, Execution, and Enablement to shared KPIs (not functional vanity metrics).

In practice, this means all functions report against the same set of cross-pillar indicators such as **pipeline coverage**, **win rate**, **ramp time**, and **customer retention**, rather than each team choosing its own metrics.

These dashboards should be designed for action:

- **Easy to Interpret**: Dashboards should be simple, visual, and intuitive, making it clear what actions are required without needing deep analysis.

- **Updated in Real Time**: Data must refresh continuously so leaders and managers can trust they are making decisions based on the latest information.

- **Accessible Across Levels**: From executives to frontline managers, everyone should see the same version of truth, tailored in depth but consistent in source.

Scorecards should highlight where the system is healthy, where risks are emerging, and where interventions are needed. By doing so, they transform data from a retrospective report into a forward-looking management tool that drives alignment and decision-making across the GTM engine.

For example, a quarterly GTM Council scorecard could look directionally like this:

Pillar	KPI Example	Status
Planning	Capacity vs. Quota Coverage	●
Execution	Pipeline Velocity	●
Execution	Win Rate	●
Enablement	Play Adoption	●
Enablement	Ramp Time	●

This allows leaders to immediately see that, say, Planning is green, Execution is yellow, and Enablement is red, triggering a focused discussion on why onboarding is behind and what actions are needed before it drags down revenue outcomes.

We'll cover a more detailed list of KPIs in a later chapter.

Example: GTM OS in Action

Let's say your win rates in mid-market are declining. A strong GTM OS enables you to respond in a way that is both fast and coordinated across functions, rather than reactive and siloed. For example:

· **Execution**: See the trend early in pipeline analytics, noticing that stage-to-stage conversion rates are dropping for opportunities over a certain deal size.

· **Enablement**: Identify skill or message gaps in call analysis; perhaps reps are consistently mishandling a new competitor objection or failing to position a recent product enhancement.

· **Planning**: Reallocate AE headcount to segments with stronger potential, adjust quota distribution, or shift Marketing spend to reinforce pipeline creation in healthier verticals.

- **Execution + Enablement**: Launch a targeted sales play (e.g., a competitive displacement playbook) and measure its lift within weeks, validating whether the intervention works.

The power of the GTM OS is that the system sees, responds, and improves in near real-time, **without waiting for QBRs or quarterly misses.** It creates a continuous improvement loop where planning adapts to execution insights, enablement closes the skill gaps, and the field gets support exactly when it's needed.

Avoiding the GTM OS Pitfalls

Avoid these common traps:

- **Over-engineering the system**: keep it simple and actionable. Leaders often try to design the "perfect" GTM OS with too many layers, tools, or dashboards. The result is complexity that slows down adoption and creates more confusion than clarity. Aim for a system that teams can actually use in their daily work.

- **Confusing visibility with alignment**: shared dashboards don't equal shared accountability. Just because everyone can see the same numbers doesn't mean they agree on what to do about them and who owns it. Alignment only happens when functions agree on ownership, handoffs, and corrective actions.

- **Running parallel rhythms**: Sales, Enablement, Marketing, and RevOps must work off one cadence. If Marketing reviews campaigns monthly, Sales reviews pipeline weekly, and Enablement runs quarterly, the rhythms never connect. A unified cadence ensures all functions inspect, adjust, and act in sync.

- **Neglecting manager enablement**: frontline managers are the true drivers of adoption. If they aren't trained, equipped, and accountable for coaching to the system, no amount of VP-level sponsorship will make it stick. Managers translate system design into daily behaviors.

Build the system **around how the business runs**, not how each function wants to operate in isolation. Think in terms of the seller and customer journey, then design governance, cadences, and enablement around those realities. The simpler and closer to the field it feels, the higher the adoption and the greater the impact.

Making the Shift: Where to Start

Before diving into the steps, it's important to recognize that implementing a GTM OS requires both discipline and sequencing. Leaders can't flip a switch and expect instant integration. The shift begins with small but high-leverage actions that create visible wins and momentum for change. These first steps form the bridge from theory to practice.

1. **Define shared KPIs across the GTM funnel**

   Go beyond vanity metrics by aligning on the handful of indicators that truly connect Planning, Execution, and Enablement. This ensures every team is driving toward the same outcomes rather than optimizing in silos.

2. **Establish a GTM Council** that includes Sales, CS, Ops, Enablement, Marketing, and Product.

   The Council becomes the forum where strategy and execution meet. It is accountable for keeping functions synchronized, addressing systemic blockers, and reallocating resources to what matters most.

3. **Map current planning and execution cadences**: where are handoffs breaking?

   Most organizations discover that their teams run on different calendars. Mapping cadences exposes disconnects and shows where feedback loops are failing, enabling the design of a unified operating rhythm.

4. **Pilot an integrated initiative** (e.g., a new product launch or segment play)

   Start small but meaningful. Piloting with a defined initiative allows you to test the GTM OS principles in a controlled environment, prove impact, and build momentum for broader rollout.

5. **Institutionalize feedback loops** from reps and frontline managers back into planning.

   This turns field experience into fuel for strategy. Regularly capture rep insights, customer reactions, and manager observations, then feed them directly into planning and enablement. The goal is to close the gap between what's happening in the field and what's being decided in the boardroom.

Think of it like upgrading your operating system, not rewriting your go-to-market strategy. By starting with these steps, you create visible wins that demonstrate the value of integration and build organizational appetite for scaling the GTM OS.

Wrap-Up: One System, One Story

Planning, Execution, and Enablement aren't separate organizational capabilities. They're parts of a unified system. When connected, they drive clarity, speed, and performance across the entire commercial organization.

You don't scale excellence through activity. You scale it through **alignment and orchestration**. That's what the GTM Operating System delivers.

In the next chapter, we'll go deeper into **GTM Maturity Models and Transformation Roadmaps**, because wherever you are today, excellence is a journey and every team needs a map.

Chapter 23: GTM Maturity and Transformation Roadmap

"You can't scale what you haven't stabilized. You can't transform what you haven't measured."

Every company wants to go faster. Very few know where they are today, let alone what "better" looks like. That's why GTM transformations stall, because teams are chasing best practices they're not ready for, or solving problems that aren't the root cause.

Transformation isn't a reorg. It's a deliberate, staged process of evolving how you **plan**, **execute**, and **enable**. And it starts by knowing your GTM maturity, so you can pick the right next moves, not just the trendy ones.

This chapter gives you a practical framework to assess where you are and plot the course to GTM excellence.

The Four Stages of GTM Maturity

Think of GTM maturity in four stages. These stages serve as a roadmap for organizations to understand not only where they currently stand, but also the milestones required to reach higher levels of sophistication. Each stage builds upon the previous one, creating a compounding effect where progress becomes more impactful and sustainable.

Stage	Description	Symptoms
Ad Hoc	GTM is reactionary, siloed, hero-dependent	Forecasts are unreliable, onboarding is inconsistent, results vary wildly by rep
Defined	Processes exist but are inconsistently applied	Planning happens, but execution and enablement are hit or miss
Integrated	Planning, Execution, and Enablement are aligned and measurable	Data-driven decisions, improving rep productivity, scalable execution
Optimized	GTM is a system: adaptive, proactive, and innovation-ready	GTM functions operate as one, drive growth predictably, and scale with efficiency

You don't move from Ad Hoc to Optimized overnight. But every step forward compounds impact. The key is knowing **how** to move through the stages:

- Moving from **Ad Hoc** → **Defined** requires discipline. Start by documenting processes, cleaning data, and enforcing consistency. It's about stabilizing the basics before scaling.

- Moving from **Defined** → **Integrated** requires alignment. Break silos by introducing shared scorecards, unified cadences, and cross-functional councils that ensure planning, execution, and enablement inform each other.

- Moving from **Integrated** → **Optimized** requires iteration. At this stage, teams use advanced analytics, AI, and field feedback to constantly refine plays, coverage, and enablement. It's about turning GTM into a living system that adapts in real time.

The journey is less about speed and more about sequencing. Trying to skip ahead leaves gaps that show up later as inefficiency or mistrust. The organizations that succeed are those that deliberately build maturity step by step, while celebrating quick wins to build momentum and trust along the way.

Assessing Your Current State

A candid cross-functional assessment will reveal where you truly are. Don't treat it as a box-checking exercise. Approach it as a diagnostic conversation that uncovers both strengths and cracks across functions. The goal is not to score yourself, but to build alignment on reality and agree on where the most pressing gaps lie. From there, the task is to translate those insights into a roadmap of action, sequencing initiatives to address the gaps while reinforcing existing strengths. This creates a consistent foundation from which transformation can move forward in a practical, phased manner. Follow some sample questions you can use to trigger discussions to identify where your GTM disciplines stand:

Planning

- Do we segment our market based on actual performance and potential, or only broad assumptions?

- Is capacity planning tied to rep productivity and TAM, or is it guesswork tied to board targets?

· Are GTM plans revisited quarterly, or are they locked for a year regardless of market signals?

Execution

· Do we have a standardized sales process used by all teams, or does each region/segment "do its own thing"?

· Are forecast calls based on disciplined criteria, or mostly on deal momentum and optimism?

· Are managers trained and accountable to inspect and coach, not just report numbers?

Enablement

· Is onboarding outcome-based, designed to shorten ramp and drive impact, or is it content-heavy and disconnected from performance?

· Do we measure enablement impact on rep productivity, or just track participation and certifications?

· Are sales plays activated, inspected, and iterated based on adoption and results?

Integration

· Do Planning, Execution, and Enablement teams operate on a shared rhythm and scorecard, or do they run parallel cadences?

· What is the cadence where these functions intersect to make decisions together?

· Is there a GTM council or operating committee with authority to resolve cross-functional issues?

· Are feedback loops from field to planning institutionalized, with visible action taken on what's heard?

The answers don't just tell you where you are. They reveal where misalignments exist. The gaps point directly to your next priorities on the maturity journey. This is how you turn assessment into action.

Building the Transformation Roadmap

Once you've assessed your maturity, build a **sequenced roadmap**. Focus on the highest-leverage gaps, not shiny initiatives. A roadmap gives clarity on what comes first, what can wait, and how to measure progress at each stage. The most effective roadmaps don't try to do everything at once, they prioritize.

Phase 1: Stabilize

The foundation. Without stable processes and data, everything else crumbles.

· Clean up pipeline data and enforce CRM stage usage so you can trust the numbers.

· Redefine the sales process with clear stage exit criteria and align manager inspection cadence to enforce it.

· Improve onboarding and roll out a small set of basic sales plays that every rep can execute consistently.

Phase 2: Systematize

Once the foundation is in place, put structure around it.

· Align capacity, territory, and quota models so resources are distributed fairly and realistically.

· Launch a shared GTM calendar and cross-functional cadences so functions are finally running on the same clock.

· Establish a set of cross-pillar KPIs that Planning, Execution, and Enablement all share accountability for.

Phase 3: Integrate

Bring the machine together and make it work as one system.

· Enable manager coaching frameworks so adoption and reinforcement are embedded in daily behavior.

· Launch predictive forecasting and pipeline dashboards that tie insights directly into operating cadences.

· Tie enablement outcomes (ramp time, play adoption) directly to rep performance and funnel metrics, proving impact.

Phase 4: Optimize

With the basics integrated, the system can now evolve and innovate.

· Roll out AI-based coaching and real-time content delivery to accelerate decision-making and skill development.

· Build GTM innovation sprints (e.g., new play pilots every quarter) to keep testing and refining approaches.

· Operationalize a "voice of the field" system into planning, ensuring frontline feedback shapes strategy and roadmap on an ongoing basis.

Navigating these stages requires patience, governance, and visible wins at each step. Resist the urge to jump straight to advanced tools before the basics are in place. Treat each phase as a layer that strengthens the one before it, and momentum will build naturally.

Leading the Transformation

This is not an RevOps project. This is a leadership challenge that requires vision, alignment, and persistence across the executive team.

Success requires:

· **Executive sponsorship**, preferably from CRO, CCO, or COO, but ideally with visible CEO endorsement to reinforce its strategic importance.

· **Dedicated transformation leads**, cross-functional, empowered, and accountable for execution, not just coordination. These leaders need the authority to break silos and make trade-offs.

· **Clear change narrative**, not just "we're evolving," but a compelling story that connects transformation to growth, customer value, and employee success. The narrative must be repeated often, tied to strategy, and reinforced in every forum.

· **Wins along the way**, every milestone should show results, not just effort. Quick wins build momentum, protect credibility, and earn investment for the harder phases of change.

If no one owns the transformation, it won't happen. If everyone owns it, it'll get diluted. Assign ownership. Treat the transformation like a product launch: build a roadmap, define success metrics, invest in adoption, and continuously iterate. That's how you make the GTM model stick and scale.

Common Pitfalls to Avoid

Every transformation journey comes with hazards. Awareness of the common traps allows leaders to avoid wasting energy or derailing momentum. Below are the most frequent mistakes organizations make during GTM maturity efforts:

- **Skipping maturity stages**: You can't optimize what you haven't integrated. Teams often jump to advanced forecasting tools or AI-based solutions without first stabilizing their pipeline data or enforcing process discipline. This creates a shiny façade with no foundation.

- **Over-relying on tools**: Technology is an enabler, not the strategy. A new CRM feature or enablement platform won't fix misaligned processes or poor coaching. Tools should accelerate well-defined workflows, not replace them.

- **Lack of enablement for the managers**: They are the linchpin; train and support them. Frontline managers translate strategy into daily behaviors. Without equipping them with frameworks, coaching guides, and accountability, even the best playbooks stall.

- **No feedback loop**: If reps aren't heard, field adoption will crater. Transformation must feel two-way, where insights from the field shape strategy, and leaders communicate how those insights were acted on. Without this, initiatives feel top-down and irrelevant.

- **Under-resourcing RevOps and Enablement**: These two functions are the backbone of the GTM OS. RevOps builds and maintains the operating system ensuring data quality, cadence alignment, and governance. Enablement equips managers and reps with the skills, plays, and coaching needed to bring strategy to life in the field. Starving either function of budget or talent guarantees the GTM OS will break under pressure: without RevOps, leaders are flying blind; without

Enablement, execution quality erodes. Both must be invested in as strategic priorities, not afterthoughts.

In short, pitfalls occur when leaders chase speed without structure, tools without process, or strategy without frontline enablement. Avoiding these traps requires patience, investment, and relentless focus on alignment.

Wrap-Up: Progress Over Perfection

GTM transformation isn't about chasing a static best practice. It's about committing to a journey of continuous improvement, quarter after quarter, year after year. The organizations that win are those that align functions around shared goals, tighten execution with discipline, and elevate Enablement from a support role to a growth engine. Progress comes from sequencing the right steps at the right time, celebrating quick wins to build confidence, and staying disciplined through setbacks. Transformation is not a finish line but a flywheel: every cycle of planning, execution, and Enablement makes the system faster, stronger, and more adaptive.

Chapter 24: Scaling GTM Across Segments and Regions

"If your GTM motion only works in one segment, it's not a system, it's a workaround."

As companies grow, complexity multiplies. What once worked for a single segment or region begins to break down across product lines, geographies, or customer tiers. Playbooks don't translate. Enablement doesn't scale. Forecasts become fragmented. And local teams start reinventing GTM in the field.

Scaling GTM requires more than replication, it requires **modular consistency**. This chapter is about how to extend your GTM operating model across the business without losing clarity, performance, or control.

Why Scaling Is Hard

Scaling a GTM system sounds straightforward... Just replicate what worked in one area across others. But in reality, the challenge is far greater. Growth introduces new variables, competing priorities, and structural complexity. Before long, what felt like a clear and simple operating model starts to strain under the weight of expansion. Leaders often underestimate how quickly consistency erodes without an intentional design.

Scaling introduces four major stressors that compound as companies grow:

· **Segment Variability**: SMB buyers want speed and simplicity; enterprise buyers demand depth, customization, and executive trust. Mid-market often sits uncomfortably in between, requiring balance. Each segment has unique expectations that force sellers to shift tone, tools, and tactics.

· **Geographic Dynamics**: Market maturity, economic climate, buyer sophistication, and competitive density vary dramatically by region. A playbook that wins in North America may flop in Asia-Pacific without localization in language, culture, and cadence.

· **Product Complexity**: As product portfolios expand, different offerings may require different motions and skill sets -i.e. transactional vs. consultative, product-led vs. sales-led, or partner-driven vs. direct- . The more diverse the portfolio, the harder it is to scale one consistent model.

· **Organizational Sprawl**: More teams, more overlays, more time zones, and more stakeholders to align. Functions start creating their own versions of GTM to "make things work," which fragments governance and makes measurement inconsistent.

The danger is clear: without a design for **modular consistency**, each region, product line, or segment builds its own "version" of GTM. This erodes efficiency, creates conflicting playbooks, and makes measuring success nearly impossible. What starts as local customization often becomes organizational sprawl, where leadership loses the ability to compare performance, replicate success, or spot systemic risk.

A scalable GTM OS anticipates these stressors and provides the shared backbone that allows local execution to flex without breaking the system.

Where to Stay Rigid vs. Where to Flex

Scaling GTM is not about choosing between centralization and localization but about knowing where you must stay rigid to preserve consistency, and where you should flex to adapt to market realities. Too much rigidity leads to brittle systems that fail to resonate locally; too much flexibility creates chaos and fragmentation. Leaders must learn to treat the GTM OS like a backbone: strong enough to provide structure, yet elastic enough to move with the body.

Stay Rigid (Non-Negotiables)	Flex (Adaptable Elements)
Sales process stages & exit criteria	Messaging and proof points tailored to buyers
Forecasting methodology & definitions	Regional campaign calendars and timing
Role definitions & accountability models	Territory mapping and account coverage
Enablement frameworks & certification	Onboarding localized to language and context
GTM cadence & governance forums	Cultural adaptations to selling style and norms

Staying rigid ensures comparability, scalability, and clarity across the business. Flexing ensures resonance with buyers and effectiveness in local markets. The art of scaling is striking this balance: rigid where measurement, governance, and consistency are critical; flexible where buyer context, culture, and execution dynamics demand adaptation.

Ultimately, this balance determines whether growth strengthens the GTM system or weakens it. High-performing organizations set clear guardrails, defining the "non-negotiables" that provide comparability, and then intentionally empower regions, segments, and product teams to innovate within those boundaries. This clarity reduces friction, accelerates adoption, and gives leaders confidence that while execution may look different in Tokyo versus Toronto, the underlying system remains intact.

Segment-Specific Design

Each segment (e.g., SMB, Mid-Market, Enterprise) demands tailored GTM mechanics. While the underlying GTM OS provides the architecture, the way it shows up in the field must reflect the realities of each segment:

- **SMB**: High-velocity, inbound-led or PLG-led, digital motion. Speed, automation, and digital engagement drive results. Metrics often focus on volume of opportunities, conversion efficiency, and digital touch effectiveness.

- **Mid-Market**: Named accounts, inside sales, scaled plays. Balance is required with enough structure to drive efficiency but enough personalization to stand out. Metrics include account coverage, pipeline creation per rep, and adoption of scaled plays.

- **Enterprise**: Long cycles, field-led, deep enablement and executive engagement. Relationships, trust, and complex deal orchestration dominate. Metrics emphasize stage conversion rates, multi-stakeholder engagement, and executive sponsor involvement.

Avoid trying to force-fit a one-size-fits-all model. Instead:

- **Share a common language and architecture** so processes and definitions are consistent across all tiers.

- **Define motion-specific metrics and coaching** so reps are measured and guided in ways relevant to their selling environment.

- **Build segment-specific onboarding and plays** that reflect the actual cycle length, buyer personas, and engagement tactics of that segment.

- **Enable managers differently by segment**: coaching an SMB team is very different from coaching an enterprise team; their rhythms, skills, and inspection points must match the motion.

You're building **variations on a theme**, not writing three different songs. The harmony comes from the shared backbone; the differentiation comes from adapting to the unique rhythm of each segment.

International Expansion and Regional Scaling

Entering new regions brings more than just translation. It requires an intentional design of how the GTM OS extends globally while adapting locally. Beyond language, leaders must consider structural, cultural, and operational dynamics:

- **Regulatory environments**: Local laws and compliance requirements can shape deal structures, data handling, and even messaging. Ignoring this can create risk or stall deals.

- **Go-to-market timing**: Economic cycles and seasonal business patterns differ across markets. Timing campaigns or launches without this context risks wasted spend or weak traction.

- **Buyer expectations**: Engagement styles vary widely. For example, relationship-based selling may dominate in parts of Asia or Latin America, while value-based or ROI-driven conversations may resonate more in North America or Europe.

- **Talent availability**: In some markets, it may be harder to recruit experienced sellers, requiring stronger enablement and tailored onboarding.

- **Channel dynamics**: In certain geographies, partner or distributor networks may be the only viable route-to-market, requiring a different operating rhythm.

Success factors for regional scaling include:

- **Hire regional leaders** who deeply understand the GTM model and can translate it into the local context without breaking the core system.

- **Run pilots before full rollouts**, proving the model in a small scale before investing heavily.

- **Localize sales plays and enablement content** so they reflect buyer language, culture, and norms while keeping structure consistent.

- **Establish a regional GTM cadence** (forecasting, reviews, play launches) that runs in sync with global rhythms but allows for local nuance.

- **Invest in cultural intelligence** training for central and regional teams to reduce friction and build trust across markets.

Think "**Global Strategy, Local Execution**", with mechanisms to track both and ensure that learning flows both ways. Regional teams inform global strategy with ground-level insight, while global teams provide consistency and discipline that keep the system scalable.

Managing Complexity Without Losing Focus

More segments and regions = More variables

Don't let that create chaos. The danger of unchecked complexity is that leaders spend more time reconciling conflicting numbers and firefighting misalignment than actually driving growth. To avoid this, companies must design with intentional simplicity, making sure the front line sees clarity, not clutter.

Protect execution quality through:

- **Standardized dashboards** across teams, with agreed-upon KPIs that roll up globally while still enabling regional drill-downs for nuance. You can be flexible on the targets for the same KPIs when matters like different maturity levels or regional market differences demand it. Dashboards must tell one story of performance that everyone can trust.

- **Central GTM Council** that governs core process and cadence, ensuring decisions on process, data, and priorities are made once and

203

cascaded consistently. Without this, each BU risks drifting into its own rhythm, creating noise instead of scale.

· **Enablement "franchises"** in regions that own local activation, not strategy, delivering training, coaching, and plays in local language and context while staying anchored to the global framework. This model balances global consistency with local resonance.

· **Unified tech stack** to consolidate data and workflows, reducing noise from disconnected tools and ensuring leaders at every level see the same truth. Tech sprawl is one of the fastest ways to erode confidence in the system.

· **Clear rules of engagement** between central and regional teams -who decides, who executes, and how escalation works- to reduce duplication and finger-pointing. These rules eliminate the gray areas that create tension and wasted effort.

Simplify wherever possible, but never at the cost of clarity in the field. The field should always experience the GTM OS as consistent, supportive, and easy to navigate. Even if behind the scenes the system is managing significant complexity, the frontline view must feel streamlined, reliable, and designed to help them win.

When to Split vs. Centralize

Not everything should scale the same way. Use these criteria to guide decisions on governance and design:

Approach	When to Use	Example
Centralize	When efficiency, consistency, or risk control is critical. Ensures comparability across the business and reduces exposure.	Keep sales process stages, compliance language, or forecasting definitions consistent globally.
Localize	When buyer expectations, language, or market maturity differ. Ensures resonance with local buyers and adapts to culture.	A mid-market playbook in the U.S. may not resonate in Japan, where relationship-building and cultural nuance are essential.
Split	When GTM maturity varies dramatically across business units. Provides flexibility where needed while retaining system tethering.	A new product line may require experimentation, while a mature enterprise segment demands more rigor and structure.

The goal is not uniformity, but **alignment on what matters, flexibility where needed**. In practice, this means codifying the backbone of GTM (process, governance, KPIs) while allowing local and business-unit leaders to adapt how plays, messaging, and coverage models show up in the field. Done right, this creates a system that is both globally consistent and locally relevant.

This section builds on the earlier discussion of **where to stay rigid vs. where to flex**. While that framework outlined the philosophical guardrails -non-negotiables versus adaptable elements- this guidance offers the **practical decision lens** for governance and design. In other words, rigid vs. flex defines the principle; centralize, localize, or split defines the action. Connecting the two ensures leaders don't just know what should stay fixed or adjustable, but also how to operationalize those choices at scale.

Wrap-Up: Scale with Purpose

Scaling GTM is not about copying a headquarters playbook. it's about architecting a system that thrives under complexity. The through line across this chapter is the discipline of **modular consistency**: building a strong backbone of non-negotiables, while empowering regions, segments, and product lines to adapt responsibly. Scaling well means balancing rigidity and flexibility, centralization and localization, efficiency and resonance.

Organizations that master this balance do more than add sellers or open new regions; they expand their **capability, alignment, and discipline**. They create one language for performance, one operating cadence for accountability, and one framework that flexes with local realities without fracturing.

As leaders, the mandate is clear: scale with purpose. Anticipate the stressors, define what must stay rigid, codify how to flex, and simplify execution for the field. That is how growth strengthens, rather than strains, the GTM system.

In the next chapter, we'll bring it all together, highlighting **the metrics that matter** most across the GTM system and how leaders can use them to steer growth with confidence.

Chapter 25: Metrics That Matter

"What gets measured gets managed. But what gets managed without alignment just creates noise."

In GTM, the wrong metrics -or the right ones viewed in isolation- can send teams chasing shadows. A metric's true value comes from its ability to inform action, connect across functions, and drive improvement. Metrics must tell a **shared story** across Planning, Execution, and Enablement, otherwise you end up with three different scoreboards and no common game plan.

Dashboards are everywhere. Yet clarity is rare.

Revenue leaders are flooded with metrics: pipeline coverage, win rate, CAC, rep attainment, CSAT, ramp time, NRR. But most organizations suffer from one of two issues: **metric overload** or **metric misalignment**. Everyone's measuring something. No one's steering with it.

The most effective GTM organizations don't just collect data; they orchestrate it. They align around a small set of metrics that act as the connective tissue across teams; metrics that start in Planning, show up in Execution, and are reinforced through Enablement. For example, pipeline coverage isn't just a planning number; it's inspected weekly in sales execution and shaped by enablement programs that accelerate pipeline creation. Ramp time isn't just an enablement stat; it directly impacts execution capacity and informs next year's planning models.

The best GTM organizations align around a focused set of **leading and lagging indicators**, tied directly to the three pillars. Metrics are not just numbers, they're the operating language of the GTM OS. This chapter gives you the blueprint to run your GTM business with precision and cohesion.

Metrics by Pillar

Before diving into the metrics, it's important to frame why this table matters. Each pillar of GTM -Planning, Execution, and Enablement- needs to be measured not in isolation, but in ways that connect directly to business outcomes. Below is a table outlining the key metrics by pillar (the list is not exhaustive), followed by brief definitions of what each means and why it matters.

Pillar	Key Metrics
Planning	· TAM/SAM/SOM Penetration · Capacity Vs. Quota Accuracy · Territory Coverage and Whitespace Analysis · Segment-Level Pipeline Creation Vs. Target
Execution	· Account Coverage · Win Rate · Quota Attainment · Breadth of Participation · Sales Cycle Length · Forecast Accuracy · Slipped Deals · Stage-To-Stage Conversion Rates
Enablement	· Ramp Time · Certification-To-Impact · Sales Play Adoption Rates · Manager Coaching Frequency and Quality · Content Usage → Deal Influence

Definitions:

· **TAM/SAM/SOM Penetration**: Percentage of the addressable market actually covered by GTM efforts. Ensures resources are aimed at winnable opportunities.

· **Capacity vs. Quota Accuracy**: Measures how well assigned quotas align with actual selling capacity. Prevents burnout or sandbagging.

- **Territory Coverage & Whitespace**: Tracks whether all market opportunities are assigned and if reps are under- or over-assigned; optimizes coverage.

- **Segment-Level Pipeline Creation vs. Target**: Assesses whether pipeline generation is keeping pace with plan across each segment.

- **Account Coverage**: Monitors whether key accounts have assigned reps and active engagement. Critical for growth and retention.

- **Win Rate**: Percentage of opportunities won vs. total pursued. Indicator of sales effectiveness.

- **Quota Attainment**: Percentage of individual or team sales quota achieved within a defined period; core measure of sales performance.

- **Breadth of Participation**: Extent to how quota attainment is distributed across the sales force rather than concentrated in a few top performers; indicates sustainability and broad team contribution.

- **Sales Cycle Length**: Average time to close deals. Measures efficiency of execution.

- **Forecast Accuracy**: Compares predicted vs. actual revenue outcomes. Tests discipline and reliability.

- **Slipped Deals**: Opportunities forecasted but not closed in time. Signals pipeline health issues.

- **Stage-to-Stage Conversion Rates**: Percentage of opportunities advancing through each stage. Pinpoints bottlenecks.

- **Ramp Time**: Time for new hires to reach full productivity. Critical for scaling capacity.

- **Certification-to-Impact**: Correlation of training/certification to measurable performance gains (i.e. win rates). Validates enablement.

- **Sales Play Adoption Rates**: Tracks how often reps use prescribed plays. Measures field alignment with strategy.

- **Manager Coaching Frequency & Quality**: Frequency and impact of coaching sessions. Drives skill reinforcement.

· **Content Usage → Deal Influence**: Measures whether content provided to reps is used in live opportunities and its impact on outcomes. Ensures enablement delivers results.

The goal is to ensure each metric ladders up to business outcomes, not just functional output. For example, content usage is interesting, but content influence on win rate is actionable.

Leading vs. Lagging Indicators

It's important to note that not all metrics behave the same way. They fall into two broad categories, each serving a different purpose in GTM management:

Lagging indicators: Reflect outcomes after the fact. They are useful for validation, showing whether strategy and execution worked, but too late to influence the current cycle.

Leading indicators: Provide early signals that allow leaders to intervene and course-correct **before** the quarter closes. They are predictive in nature and help managers steer the business in real time.

Follow some examples:

Type	Example Metrics	Purpose / Why It Matters
Lagging	Revenue, Win Rate, Quota Attainment, NRR	Validates long-term performance; confirms if the strategy worked
Leading	Pipeline Created, Stage Conversion Rates, Play Adoption, Coaching Cadence, CS Health Coverage	Offers early-warning signals; allows intervention and increases the chance of success

Best practice: Maintain a healthy mix of both but focus weekly operating rhythms on leading indicators. Use lagging metrics in monthly/ quarterly reviews to validate strategy.

Dashboards that Drive Action

Most dashboards fail for one reason: they inform, but don't direct.

Dashboards should be more than static reports. They must be **operational tools** that guide decisions and actions. They should create a bridge between numbers on a screen and conversations in the room.

Instead of simply reporting history, effective dashboards shape the narrative of what needs to happen next.

To make them effective:

· Assign **clear ownership** so someone is accountable for upkeep and usage.

· Show **trendlines** to reveal progress over time, not just snapshots.

· Highlight **exceptions and variances** that require immediate action.

· Link directly to **weekly, monthly, and quarterly cadences** so insights fuel timely discussions and reviews.

· Embed **context and commentary** so leaders don't just see what happened but understand why.

· Connect to **playbooks or actions** so a flagged issue translates into the next best step for managers and reps.

The best dashboards prompt action the moment they are reviewed, transforming visibility into execution. They stop being rear-view mirrors and become steering wheels for the business, ensuring that data becomes dialogue and dialogue becomes decisive action.

Boardroom vs. Field Views

Different audiences require different views of the same truth. The way metrics are presented should match the lens and decision-making needs of each group. Below is a comparison showing how perspectives vary across audiences:

Audience	Focused Metrics & Views	Purpose / Why It Matters
Boardroom	Bookings vs. plan, CAC/payback periods, NRR/GRR, coverage ratios, forecast confidence	Provides a strategic, financial-level view; enables resource allocation and investor confidence
Field	Stage quality, rep activity vs. outcomes, coaching cadence adherence, progression velocity	Guides frontline managers and reps; helps identify execution gaps and coaching needs

| Enablement | Ramp trends, certification-to-performance correlation, sales play performance by cohort | Demonstrates the impact of enablement efforts on sales outcomes; links enablement efforts to performance |

These perspectives ensure that each level of the organization sees metrics in the context that matters most to their decisions. They also reinforce alignment: while the views differ, they are all derived from the same source of truth.

GTM Health Scorecard

A **simple, color-coded scorecard** -green for healthy, yellow for at-risk, red for urgent- can focus attention where it matters most. By aligning this scorecard to the shared KPIs across Planning, Execution, and Enablement, you create a single visual cue for organizational health. This turns metrics into a living management tool rather than a static report.

Example GTM Health Scorecard:

Pillar	KPI	Target	Current	Status
Planning	Territory Coverage %	95%	92%	🟡
Execution	Win Rate	30%	33%	🟢
Execution	Forecast Accuracy (within ±5%)	90%	84%	🟡
Enablement	Ramp Time (days)	90	105	🔴
Enablement	Sales Play Adoption %	85%	88%	🟢

This kind of visual makes it immediately clear where leadership should focus energy and resources in the next operating cycle.

Wrap-Up: Manage the System, Not the Parts

GTM organizations don't win by tracking everything; they do by aligning on a few critical metrics that matter most. The goal isn't to be data-driven for its own sake, but to be insight-driven, turning data into decisions that accelerate performance.

When planning, execution, and enablement metrics are tied together, your business becomes not just predictable, but scalable.

When metrics are managed as a unified system rather than disconnected parts, they generate clarity, focus, and action.

When every number tells a story and points to a next step, you transform from being metric-heavy to being truly insight-driven.

This cohesion is the essence of GTM excellence. In the final chapter, we'll look forward at how GTM is evolving, and what leaders must do now to stay ahead.

Chapter 26: The Future of GTM

"The GTM of tomorrow isn't more tools or more headcount. It's sharper strategy, cleaner execution, and faster feedback."

To illustrate why change is necessary, consider the case of a software company selling into mid-market enterprises. A decade ago, its reps could succeed with cold calls, booked demos, and a linear funnel leading to closed deals. Today, those same buyers research extensively online before ever speaking to sales, expect pricing transparency, and compare solutions across peer reviews. AI-driven tools now highlight which accounts are showing intent and even draft personalized outreach, while customer success teams join early to ensure adoption and expansion are built into the initial sale.

This scenario makes the **case for change** clear: the old funnel playbook can't keep up with how buyers move and make decisions. GTM must be dynamic, integrated, and orchestrated.

In other words, the GTM playbook can no longer be static. It must evolve into a **dynamic system** that is constantly sensing, learning, and adapting. The emphasis is shifting from brute force (i.e. more calls, more reps, more content) toward precision, personalization, and agility. Organizations that fail to adapt risk being left behind.

Before diving into the specific shifts, it's helpful to summarize the biggest forces reshaping GTM today. The table below highlights the **key change drivers**, what looks different now compared to a decade ago, and why each shift matters.

Change Driver	What's Different Now	Why It Matters
Buyer Expectations	Buyers research extensively online, expect transparency, and rely on peer reviews	Sales teams must engage later in the cycle with more tailored, value-driven conversations
Technological Disruption	AI tools surface intent data, personalize outreach, and coach reps in real time	Organizations that adopt AI gain speed, precision, and scalability in their GTM efforts
Competitive Intensity	Markets are more crowded, cycles more complex, and multiple channels converge	A static playbook fails; only dynamic, adaptive systems can keep pace with fast-moving rivals

The takeaway is clear: GTM leaders of the future won't win by just scaling. They'll win by knowing how to **adapt, integrate, and orchestrate** across teams, tools, and channels. This chapter explores what is changing, why it matters, and how leaders can prepare to stay ahead.

Shifts Underway

The trends highlighted in the table above are not theoretical; they are already reshaping how GTM teams must operate. Each represents a transition from the way organizations historically managed GTM to a new model designed for today's realities.

From	To	What Changes	Why It Matters
Linear Funnel	**Continuous Flywheel**	Shifts focus from acquisition as the sole driver to expansion and retention rivaling new business	GTM must design around the full lifecycle, not just new logo wins, making Customer Success a growth engine
Coverage	**Conversion**	Moves from headcount and activity volume as measures to efficiency, conversion, and quality	Productivity per rep, per segment, and per motion becomes the true measure of success
Enablement	**Embedded Intelligence**	Evolves from static content portals to AI-powered assistants, real-time guidance, and contextual nudges	The best sellers are those who leverage machine support for smarter, faster selling
Siloed Functions	**Revenue Orchestration**	Transitions from separate planning, execution, and enablement functions to integrated operating threads	Organizations collapse functional handoffs in favor of unified pods, missions, and GTM squads

These shifts are underway because of a convergence of buyer expectations, technological acceleration, and heightened competition. Together, they point toward a more connected, ecosystem-driven future.

For leaders, the question becomes: where to start? Not every shift can be tackled at once, and prioritization matters. A practical approach is to:

- **Anchor in the buyer**: Focus first on aligning with how your buyers prefer to engage.

- **Leverage quick wins**: Introduce AI tools or process changes that provide immediate lift in productivity.

- **Orchestrate cross-functionally**: Break down silos by creating shared scorecards and integrated operating rhythms.

By sequencing the journey in this way, GTM leaders avoid being overwhelmed and instead build momentum toward transformation. Ultimately, GTM leaders must think in terms of ecosystems, not functions, if they are to remain relevant and competitive.

How AI Is Reshaping GTM

AI won't replace the human seller, but it will **force the seller to evolve**.

For sellers, AI represents both empowerment and disruption. It automates tasks that used to consume hours and provides insights that sharpen execution. Yet it also raises the bar: reps must learn to interpret AI-driven insights, differentiate themselves where machines cannot, and build trust that algorithms alone cannot secure.

For RevOps and Enablement teams, the challenge is even sharper. They must become the architects of AI integration, ensuring that tools are not just deployed but adopted, trusted, and aligned to workflows. Without discipline, AI can overwhelm sellers with alerts and data, creating noise instead of clarity.

Expect to see capabilities like:

- **Automated call analysis** identifying coachable moments in real time

- **Smart forecasting engines** that outperform human judgment

- **Personalized outreach and content generation** at scale

- **Dynamic sales play surfacing** based on opportunity context

- **Continuous readiness assessments** through behavioral data

- **Market & Account Targeting** with ICP refinement, propensity scoring, and dynamic segmentation

- **Pipeline & Forecasting** with health diagnostics, scenario planning, and AI-driven accuracy improvements

- **Sales Execution** enhanced by buyer engagement intelligence, call/meeting analysis, and playbook automation

- **Revenue Enablement** delivering personalized training, real-time coaching, and knowledge retrieval

- **Compensation & Territory Design** with AI-enabled quota setting, territory optimization, and incentive simulations

- **Customer Success & Expansion** with churn prediction, expansion signal detection, and dynamic health scoring

- **GTM Analytics & Governance** including anomaly detection, attribution clarity, and rhythm optimization

To harness these shifts, future GTM organizations will need new capabilities:

- **Data literacy across the field** so reps and managers can interpret and act on AI insights

- **AI governance in RevOps** to manage data quality, bias, and adoption

- **Performance enablement platforms** that act as AI control towers, embedding insights directly into daily workflows

- **Change management muscles** to help sellers adapt mindsets and habits alongside tools

The Enablement function of the future won't be a training team. It will be a **performance AI control tower**; designing, governing, and scaling the human + machine partnership that defines modern GTM.

AI Readiness Checklist for GTM Leaders

To prepare, leaders should assess their current maturity against a practical readiness checklist:

Dimension	Questions to Ask	Why It Matters
Seller Readiness	Do reps know how to use AI insights in conversations? Are they trained to differentiate where humans add unique value?	Ensures sellers remain trusted advisors rather than over-relying on automation
RevOps Governance	Is there clear ownership of AI tools, data pipelines, and model governance?	Prevents data overload, bias, and lack of adoption
Enablement Integration	Are AI-driven insights embedded into workflows, playbooks, and coaching cadences?	Aligns enablement with execution so insights turn into behavior change
Data Infrastructure	Is data accurate, unified, and accessible across systems?	AI only works as well as the data feeding it
Change Management	Do managers and reps have support to adapt to new ways of working?	Builds confidence and adoption, minimizes resistance

This checklist helps leaders identify gaps and prioritize investments, so AI becomes an accelerator, not a distraction.

What Won't Change

Even as AI transforms workflows and new technologies reshape how sellers engage buyers, certain fundamentals will remain constant. These enduring truths act as the bedrock on which all innovation must rest.

- **Buyer trust** still wins deals. Relationships and credibility cannot be automated; they are earned through integrity, consistency, and delivering value.

- **Value articulation** still beats product pitching. No matter how advanced the tools, buyers respond to clear articulation of outcomes, not feature lists.

- **Manager coaching** still scales execution. AI can highlight opportunities, but only human managers can contextualize feedback, motivate, empower, and develop skills in the field.

· **Planning discipline** still drives efficiency. Dynamic tools help, but without disciplined planning cycles and resource alignment, organizations will drift.

Tech will evolve. Markets will shift. But the fundamentals of GTM - aligning teams, focusing effort, executing with intent- aren't going anywhere. In fact, these foundations become even more critical as complexity rises, serving as the anchor while organizations navigate rapid change.

What GTM Leaders Must Do Next

So, the natural question is: what should leaders actually do will all this?

To stay ahead, GTM leaders must focus on five imperatives that bring these insights to life:

· **Audit your GTM system for integration gaps**: Evaluate how well Planning, Execution, and Enablement connect. Misalignment here leads to three different scoreboards and fragmented performance.

· **Invest in RevOps and Enablement as strategic multipliers**: Treat these not as support functions but as the architects of orchestration, ensuring insights, AI, and processes translate into field execution.

· **Redesign cadences and scorecards for real-time decision-making**: Move away from lagging quarterly reviews and build operating rhythms where leading indicators are inspected weekly.

· **Pilot AI in small, high-leverage workflows**: Start where AI can quickly add value -deal reviews, call planning and scoring, surfacing next-best sales plays- then scale once adoption is proven.

· **Train frontline managers for the next era of selling**: Equip managers to coach in an AI-enabled world, balancing machine insights with human judgment and leadership.

The future GTM leader is not confined to one discipline. They are part strategist (defining direction), part operator (designing systems), and part technologist (harnessing AI and tools). Their role is to orchestrate the entire commercial engine as a cohesive whole.

Final Word: GTM as a Leadership Discipline

This book has offered frameworks, checklists, and playbooks. But at its core, *From Strategy to Revenue* is about **leadership**. It's about creating clarity where there's noise. Building systems where there's chaos. Driving outcomes through people, not just process.

The path forward requires leaders who can connect strategy with execution and enablement, who see beyond functional silos, and who can orchestrate a dynamic, adaptive GTM system. It also requires courage; the courage to experiment, to rethink outdated practices, and to embrace AI and data-driven tools while keeping people at the center.

You don't need to be perfect. You need to be committed: committed to learning, to iterating, and to unifying diverse teams behind a common purpose. Leadership in GTM is less about having all the answers and more about cultivating the conditions where teams can discover, align, and act with speed.

Because the organizations that win the GTM game in the next decade won't be the ones that try harder. They'll be the ones that operate smarter, adapting to buyers, harnessing technology, reinforcing fundamentals, and developing their people.

That journey doesn't begin later. **It starts now… With you.**

About the Author

Juan Ignacio Elias is a senior leader in Revenue Operations, Go-to-Market Strategy, and Sales Excellence with more than two decades of experience leading global organizations across SaaS, technology, and industrial sectors. His leadership career spans roles at Paychex, Workday, Accenture, Shell and Ford, as well as advisory and consulting work with high-growth companies seeking to scale their commercial operations.

Throughout his career, Juan has built a reputation for transforming complex go-to-market challenges into practical systems that deliver measurable impact. He has led initiatives that accelerated sales onboarding by 40%, lifted win rates by 25%, and driven multi-million-dollar savings in back-office revenue services, as well as designing a commercial excellence procurement program that yielded $6 billion in savings globally. His ability to blend strategy, execution, and enablement has made him a trusted partner to executives and sales leaders around the world.

Juan is passionate about closing the gap between GTM planning, frontline sales execution, and revenue enablement, a theme that inspired *From Strategy to Revenue*. Through real-world case studies, proven frameworks, and actionable tools, he equips leaders to align resources with precision, create execution discipline, and enable their teams to perform at their best.

Originally from Argentina and now based in Houston, Texas, Juan is also a mentor and advisor on the future of Revenue Operations and the evolving role of Sales Enablement. Outside of his professional work, he enjoys spending time with his family, flying as a volunteer Angel Flight pilot, practicing Taekwondo, and mentoring the next generation of commercial leaders.

Connect with Juan on LinkedIn:
https://www.linkedin.com/in/juanielias/

Glossary of Acronyms

This glossary compiles all acronyms used throughout the book, with clear definitions for quick reference.

AE – Account Executive

A quota-carrying sales professional responsible for closing business, typically managing opportunities through the full sales cycle.

AI – Artificial Intelligence

Technology that simulates human intelligence in machines, enabling tasks such as learning, reasoning, problem-solving, and decision-making.

ARR – Annual Recurring Revenue

A key SaaS metric representing the yearly value of subscription revenue contracted.

ASP – Average Selling Price

The average revenue earned per closed deal; useful for understanding deal size trends.

BANT – Budget, Authority, Need, Timeline

A sales qualification framework used to assess a prospect's readiness to buy based on budget, decision authority, business need, and timing.

BU – Business Unit

A division within an organization that operates as a separate entity with its own strategy, operations, and P&L responsibility.

CAC – Customer Acquisition Cost

The total cost of acquiring a new customer, including Sales and Marketing expenses.

CCO – Chief Customer Officer

An executive responsible for customer success, adoption, retention, and expansion.

CEO – Chief Executive Officer

The most senior executive in a company, responsible for overall corporate strategy and decision-making.

CHRO – Chief Human Resources Officer

An executive overseeing HR strategy, policies, and talent management.

CFO – Chief Financial Officer

An executive responsible for managing financial strategy, reporting, and risk.

COO – Chief Operating Officer

An executive overseeing day-to-day business operations.

CRM – Customer Relationship Management

Software that manages a company's interactions with customers and prospects, tracking Sales, Marketing, and support activities.

CRO – Chief Revenue Officer

The executive responsible for all revenue-generating functions, often overseeing Sales, Marketing, and Customer Success.

CS – Customer Success

A function focused on ensuring customers achieve value, adopt solutions, and renew or expand contracts.

CSAT – Customer Satisfaction Score

A metric that measures customer satisfaction with a product, service, or interaction.

CSM – Customer Success Manager

A role dedicated to customer adoption, value realization, and retention.

CTA – Call to Action

A prompt encouraging a buyer to take a specific next step in the Sales or Marketing journey.

DSR – Digital Sales Room

A secure, collaborative digital environment where sellers and buyers engage around proposals, resources, and deal-related materials.

EBITDA – Earnings Before Interest, Taxes, Depreciation, and Amortization

A financial metric used to assess a company's operating performance by excluding non-operational expenses.

EOQ – End of Quarter

The closing period of a fiscal quarter, often marked by intense focus on closing deals to meet targets.

ERP – Enterprise Resource Planning

Integrated software used to manage core business processes such as Finance, HR, supply chain, and operations.

GTM – Go-To-Market

The strategy and set of actions a company uses to deliver its products or services to customers and achieve competitive advantage.

GRR – Gross Revenue Retention

The percentage of recurring revenue retained from existing customers, excluding expansions.

HCM – Human Capital Management

A category of enterprise software that manages HR processes including recruiting, payroll, benefits, and workforce planning.

HR – Human Resources

The function responsible for managing people within an organization, including recruitment, performance, training, and compliance.

HRBP – Human Resources Business Partner

An HR professional embedded within business units to align people strategy with business strategy.

ICP – Ideal Customer Profile

A description of the type of company that is most likely to buy, benefit from, and stay with your product or service.

IT – Information Technology

The department responsible for managing technology infrastructure, systems, and security within an organization.

KPI – Key Performance Indicator

A measurable value that indicates how effectively an individual, team, or organization is achieving objectives.

LMS – Learning Management System

A platform for delivering, tracking, and managing training and learning programs.

LPI – Leading Performance Indicator

Forward-looking metrics that predict future outcomes and performance.

LXP – Learning Experience Platform

A modern learning system focused on personalized, user-driven experiences.

MAP – Mutual Action Plan

A collaborative document between buyer and seller that outlines key milestones, responsibilities, and timelines required to achieve a successful purchase and implementation.

MEDDICC – Metrics, Economic Buyer, Decision Criteria, Decision Process, Identify Pain, Champion, Competition

A sales qualification framework used to ensure complex B2B opportunities are thoroughly vetted across all critical decision factors.

MQL – Marketing Qualified Lead

A prospect identified by Marketing as having demonstrated enough engagement or fit to be passed to Sales for further qualification.

NPS – Net Promoter Score

A metric measuring customer loyalty and likelihood to recommend a product or service.

NRR – Net Revenue Retention

The percentage of recurring revenue retained and expanded from existing customers, including upgrades, cross-sells, and churn.

OS – Operating System

In the GTM context, a structured framework that integrates planning, execution, and enablement into a cohesive rhythm.

PEO – Professional Employer Organization

A firm that provides comprehensive HR outsourcing services such as payroll, benefits, compliance, and risk management.

PLG – Product-Led Growth

A business model where product usage drives customer acquisition, retention, and expansion.

PMO – Project Management Office

A centralized team or department that defines and maintains project management standards, governance, and best practices.

QBR – Quarterly Business Review

A structured meeting where leadership reviews business performance, pipeline, goals, and execution priorities every quarter.

RevOps – Revenue Operations

The function that unifies Sales, Marketing, and Customer Success operations to align data, processes, and insights across the revenue engine.

ROI – Return on Investment

A performance metric evaluating the profitability of an investment relative to its cost.

RPA – Robotic Process Automation

Technology that uses software robots or "bots" to automate repetitive, rules-based back-office tasks.

SAL – Sales Accepted Lead

A lead that has been reviewed and formally accepted by sales from Marketing for further engagement.

SAM – Serviceable Available Market

The segment of the total addressable market that your company's products and services can serve.

SDR – Sales Development Representative

A role focused on prospecting, qualifying leads, and booking meetings for Account Executives.

SEP – Sales Enablement Platform

A system that delivers content, tracks usage, and surfaces analytics to drive sales effectiveness.

SKO – Sales Kickoff

An annual or biannual event that aligns sales teams on strategy, priorities, and plays for the year.

SMB – Small and Medium-Sized Business

A customer segment defined by smaller company size and typically faster sales cycles.

SOM – Serviceable Obtainable Market

The portion of the serviceable available market that your company can realistically capture.

SPIFF – Sales Performance Incentive Fund (or Formula)

A short-term incentive, typically monetary, used to motivate sales reps to achieve specific goals or sell particular products.

SPM – Sales Performance Management

Software and processes used to manage sales planning, incentives, territory alignment, and performance tracking.

SQL – Sales Qualified Lead

A prospect that has been vetted by Sales or Marketing and deemed ready for direct sales engagement.

TAM – Total Addressable Market

The total revenue opportunity available if a company captured 100% of the market for its product or service.

UI – User Interface

The means by which a person interacts with software or a system, including screens, buttons, and design elements.

VP – Vice President

An executive title typically responsible for leading a function, department, or regional business unit.